S0-BYX-958

GOLF & me
playing for knee

by
Roly Lamontagne

olivemount™
press
Carlsbad, CA 92009

GOLF & me
playing for knee

1st edition
1 December 2003
First Printing

ISBN 097156383-7

Printed in the U.S.A.

DEDICATION

to Bev and Michelle

the best wife and daughter
a man could have

Roly Lamontagne introduced to me the idea of playing for knee on the golf course. Although I had played junior golf at a competitive level, played in occasional open events and participated in club tournaments, I never really felt pressure in golf until I played for knee. It is personal match play with a kick to it.

The loser must kneel, clutch the victor's putter like a conqueror's swordblade, bow his head, and recite these words: "It was a privilege to be beaten by a better golfer and a superior human being."

And this must be done at the back of the 18th green in full view of playing partners, bystanders, and the clubhouse crowd.

One of my greatest golf memories is Roly beaten and obliged to give me knee on the 18th green at Aviara in La Costa. His boss and some friends laughingly watched from a clubhouse balcony.

One of my most humiliating experiences in golf...and I have more than a few to choose from...was having to give Roly knee on the back of the 18th green at Poppy Hills in Monterey. A whole host of my clients watched with glee from the clubhouse as Roly thoughtfully placed his own towel on the ground so I wouldn't get grass stains on my pants.

Playing for knee has taught me a new dimension of this game; it cannot be conquered, but it can be thoroughly enjoyed.

— a Golfer who enjoys playing for knee

Introduction

Welcome to the Roly Lamontagne memorial course. I built it myself, not always by design. It will take you through my life and love affair with golf in 18 chapters. There are lots of ups and downs, hazards and traps, penalties and rewards...and there are also a lot of laughs.

Golf is a funny game. It's like life. It gives moments of exceptional elation and wonderful self-satisfaction, and it frustrates and depresses even the greatest players. Just when everything is going great and you think you've mastered it, things can change in an instant, cause you to fail, humble you. I've learned a lot from it.

Like life, golf is a game you play and control by yourself. No one else hits your ball. The conditions change from day to day...sometimes from hole to hole. So do your abilities. You might lose today, but there's always tomorrow and a new round and a hopefully better swing.

And there are no real losers. No matter how you play, there's being outdoors, sunshine, a day of adventure and endeavor...and most importantly, the enjoyment of the people you play with, friends, good-natured ribbing, and the strange and wonderful things that happen only on a golf course. Golf is a good time and a good part of any day, win or lose.

No matter how seriously it's played, the game produces many truly funny moments and should be played with a sense of humor. That's the heart of what I'm trying to tell you within these pages. Enjoy it, and use it to expand your enjoyment of life.

First on the tee.

Golf is a child's game made difficult by adults.

That may be the best definition of golf I've ever heard. And the older I get, the truer it becomes. Now I'm just your ordinary old average weekend golfer, but I've had the good fortune to play and enjoy the game at some higher levels of accomplishment. And, like thousands of other golfers, I started by caddying.

I was eight years old and the smallest caddy at the Brockton Country Club in Massachusetts. The members' bags were as big as I was; I could have used them as sleeping chambers. At first, I caddied more for the money I earned than for any love of the game. I'd ride my bike up to the Country Club early in the morning, go into the caddy shack, hold my own with the older boys, and wait to get called to pack a bag when my turn came. I remember that I made a buck for making the loop; it was the start of my financial career. I enjoyed the entire experience. It provided a place to go and a means of making some money. It gave me a mission and an identity, very important when you're eight years old.

I got a reputation for dependability and awareness, and the reputation got me a steady caddying job for Mr. Bell in a regular foursome. I packed Mr. Bell's bag, held the flag, and kept score. I also ran in between nines to get snacks while the four men went downstairs for liquid refreshments. That foursome was always good to me.

Life was good. I spent the next ten years caddying and developing my own game. I'll bet I was the only kid caddying who gave lessons to my foursome. Ultimately, I became a very good player and qualified for the Francis Ouimet caddy scholarship when I was eighteen; it helped pay my way through college. I owe my direction in life to my start as a caddy.

Apart from golf, my athletic career in other sports has always been cursed. That's what started me. Because of a baseball injury, I decided to play golf until I mended. My Little League team improved without me, and I found the true sport of my life. As one door shuts, another opens.

I still remember the first time I actually played. It was a Monday, normally designated as "caddy day" because few members played on Monday morning. The course was ours from sun-up to noon, but not a moment longer. For anyone who has never caddied or been subjected to the restrictions of caddy day, that means you have to be finished and off the course by the stroke of twelve. That means, when caddies play, they don't mess around.

We could get in almost 36 holes in that six-hour period. We hit, and we ran. If we whiffed, we threw and we ran. If we needed water, we ran to the drinking fountain, we drank, and we ran. If we needed to pee, we peed on the course behind a bush, and we ran. God forbid that we had to stop for anything more; if we did, it meant we might miss a hole or two. It was golf, but it was golf in a speeded-up *Our Gang* movie. Get the picture?

There I was, a skinny little eight-year-old who decided to play golf because he was on the injured reserve list in Little League. And I was equipped with six irons: a driving iron, mashie, spade mashie, niblick, spade niblick, and something that looked like today's wedge. Rounding out my collection was a blade putter, a pretty mahogany-colored spoon, and a persimmon driver whose steel shaft had more flex than a strand of cooked spaghetti. Most of these clubs were hickory-shafted; I believe that's where the nickname "sticks" came from to describe clubs. All of mine were already ancient, and the only places they can be seen today are in collectors' displays.

My bag was a real beauty, khaki canvas with several patched areas, patches courtesy of the local cobbler. The bag had no spine, so if I put it down the wrong way, it dropped its trousers. The bag strap was an old belt that the inventive tailor had attached for me.

I was ready for the round with balls I had found on the course. That was another source of revenue. I constantly hunted for golf balls to sell for a nickel apiece. We got a dime for an especially cherry, very white ball. The ball I had selected to hit first was yellowish. Golf balls get yellowish when you wash them and they soak too long in the water and bleach. They turn yellowish and the paint dissolves, but they're okay.

For the occasion, my dad had given me a new ball, a Dunlop 65 from Great Britain. It was wrapped in tissue and sealed with a foil sticker, and it had been in his drawer for at least twenty years. I elected to use it at the right time later in the round when I had gained more confidence in my ability not to lose it.

Anyway, there I was on the first tee as a player for the very first time. Armed and dangerous...ready to play...carrying my own bag. I had it all!

The big guys went first, and the little kids went last; otherwise, we'd have been mowed down as surely as if we'd been caught in an artillery barrage. I was playing with a kid whose parents lived by the eighth hole. Little Johnny Adams was a peanut like me, but he was already a player, the seasoned veteran of at least two caddy days.

Finally, our turn came. After Johnny teed off, I pulled out a previously-driven, splintered tee and carefully placed my Clorox-yellowed ball on it. Johnny Adams stood to my right, watching my preparations to hit my very first shot ever. What a moment! I can still see it as though I was standing outside myself. The little golfer takes the driver back and swings at a low, outside pitch with his best Little League baseball swing. He shanks it sideways and almost takes off little Johnny's head. Despite near-decapitation, Johnny starts running down the fairway. I scoot sideways, get my ball, and throw it like a baseball down the fairway. I too am off and running. Gosh almighty! Life was great.

At about the fourth hole, after I had honed my skills, I unwrapped the Dunlop 65 with great ceremony and teed it up. When I hit it, the old new ball exploded. Only it wasn't a trick exploding ball; it was just too old. That's how I learned that golf balls didn't age very well. Despite that disintegration, my first round was a success. I loved it.

My running start was the beginning. Every day got better. Now when I was caddying, I could tell Mr. Bell, "Yeah, I've been over there, and it's a tough shot. Here's what I'd do." For an eight-year-old peanut, it just doesn't get any better than that.

That first time off the tee and another moment after I won a city tournament put me on the path to becoming a professional golfer. The win got my name in the local newspaper. *The Brockton Enterprise* posted news and sports results in their building's huge glass windows. Downtown, people paused to look in the windows and learn the sports results for the Red Sox, Celtics, Bruins, and golf. The year I led the annual Brockton City Open, beating pros and top amateurs from the area, the results were put up in headline type on galley paper in a prominent place in the windows. The headline announced **Roly Lamontagne leads Open.** That was it; I was destined to try the PGA Tour.

Junior achievement.

Progress in golf is measured in several ways: by your scores, by your own satisfaction with your ball-striking, and by your achievements in competitive events playing against your peers. Classifications and tournaments are set up by age groupings. My immediate love of the game and competitive nature prompted me to test myself at every opportunity.

Junior Golf was a real kick. Back when I was a kid, Junior Golf didn't involve playing in national events or being driven around by your mom or dad. My parents couldn't afford to take a sabbatical to act as my chauffeur.

I'm talking about local Junior Golf with new-found buddies. That's where I started to meet some truly funny guys, and it was the beginning of my crazy collection of golf characters.

Junior Golf was in itself a lesson in life. For example, it forced me to sharpen my math skills as well as my ball striking. I played with a number of kids who had trouble keeping their scores straight because they were somewhat wishful when it came to counting. My initial reaction was to wonder if I wanted to compete with a bunch of kids who kept questionable scores. Most of them were more proficient with a pencil than they were with a putter. However, as I progressed, I found that the majority of the Junior players were honorable and fun to be with. We finally weeded out the weak mathematicians and got to a point where our abilities were the only real reason for winning.

My game came around, and I became the local Junior Junior Champion, for boys under fourteen. As a fourteen-year-old, I won the Brockton Junior Championship. It was for boys up to eighteen years old. I was learning. Then, out of the blue, in 1957, when I was seventeen, I won the Massachusetts Junior Golf Championship. I followed it up by becoming the 1957 Massachusetts Junior Chamber of Commerce Champion. That was quite a year for me.

The Massachusetts Junior Championship involved seven rounds of golf. There were two medal rounds to set the field at 32 qualifiers. That meant that to qualify, I had to shoot one of the 32 lowest scores for the 36 holes. That got me in the tournament. Then the qualifying Juniors had to go through five rounds of match play to determine a winner. In match play, score is kept by the hole...won, lost or tied...against an individual opponent. That meant half the field was eliminated each day. If you lost, you were out.

I was in a fog all week, playing beyond my previous abilities. I knew I was pretty good within Brockton, but not that good for the entire State of Massachusetts. The Juniors from the Boston area got all the press in the papers, but I won my first three matches.

Each day I won meant that I was late for work at Bob & Ken's Restaurant, where I was a soda jerk behind the counter. I'd work until approximately 1:00 in the morning, go home and get three hours sleep, then drive 50 miles to the golf course where the tournament was being held. Little did I know then that I would repeat that experience on a much larger scale later in my life. Sometimes Mr. Mague, my Jaycee chaperone, would drive me, but I never got more than three or four hours sleep. The sleep deprivation must have helped my young game because I kept winning.

In my semifinal match, I beat Jay Dolan III, a fine player and the defending champion. I made seven birdies in 16 holes and beat him three and two (three holes up with two to play). Ever hear the expression "Golf makes friends"? Jay and I became good friends, and later he became my sponsor and big brother in our sports fraternity at Rollins College.

The championship match put me against Peter Haigh, a Junior from the local area, and I won, five and four. In the match, I made five birdies. That added up to 12 birdies in my last 30 holes of competition!

I was on top of the world. Wow, a 17-year-old kid being interviewed by the *Boston Globe*, the *Boston Herald*, and the local Quincy newspaper! Called into the clubhouse for a telephone interview from the *Brockton Enterprise*. Receiving a time-honored trophy. This was the big-time. I was there.

After the dizzying award ceremony and the drive home to Brockton, when I arrived at our house on Carroll Avenue, there were home-made signs by neighborhood friends: **WELCOME HOME - ROLY - STATE CHAMP!**

Some memories of winning stay with you forever. Trophy in hand, I ran into the house and found my father downstairs in the cellar. I remember that he was sweeping the floor, and I can see him in my mind as clearly as if it was yesterday.

"Dad! Dad! I won!" He said nothing. "Dad! Dad! I won," I said again.

He slowly stopped sweeping, stared at me for a moment, and said, "Roly, when you left home this morning, you were a good kid. Are you still that same good kid?" I stood in silence, not knowing what to say. The trophy was now down by my side. He put down the broom, walked over and put his arms around me. Then he said, "I'm really proud of you...not just for winning...but for who you are."

Neither of us said anything else. I prize having won the Junior championships, but I treasure that moment with my dad above anything I've ever won.

That same year, I was selected with three other boys to represent the Commonwealth of Massachusetts in the International Junior Chamber of Commerce Championship at Columbus, Ohio. It was to be played at Ohio State University. I'd come a long way since almost beheading little Johnny Adams with my first shot.

For almost two weeks, we were the guests of Ohio State in their stadium dorms. Each dorm had 20 beds accommodating four state teams of four boys each and four unfortunate chaperones. Those chaperones were ill-prepared for the antics of 16 uncaged teenaged boys, full of adrenaline, testosterone, and themselves.

The first night at the Ohio State Student Union, after the opening dinner and an address by Mr. Bobby Jones, the leading light of golf, the sliding doors were opened to present 200 cheerleaders and local high school sorority girls. They were all beautiful. I actually corralled a date. It didn't get any better than that! What an evening! A visit with one of the greatest golfers of all time, then 200 beautiful girls concentrated in one area. Count 'em, 200 beautiful girls. Turn the testosteroned animals loose. Forget the chaperones. Bed check?!! Rats! We had to be back in our dorm by 11:00 PM without fail, without female company, and without any funny stuff. It was a tribute to our dedication to golf, even more to our adult supervision and security, that we all made it back on time; at least my dorm did.

But boys will be boys. At about midnight, from total darkness, a wet towel whistled across the room. Unerringly, the missile found a fresh, freckled face that had been fast asleep. It became a team thing and took on a wild, wet life of its own.

On arriving, we had each been issued eight white towels for shower use. Check my math...16 boys times eight towels apiece equals 128 wet white towels flying through the night air. As far as I know, this was the first interstate liquid missile launch. To this day, I regard it as a hormonal release...from seeing Bobby Jones in person. Two chaperones shut off the water in the bathrooms. The other two slept through the crisis; they had partaken of a social refreshment or two while they watched us woo and wow the wonderful young women of Ohio earlier in the evening. And here's a towel factoid to end this soggy story: a significant number of my dorm-mates turned in seven towels used in battle and only one used in bath. Boys will be boys.

The whole thing was one of the greatest experiences of my life. A belated thank you to the International Junior Chamber of Commerce, even though I didn't win. Oh, by the way...a kid named Nicklaus won it.

Just imagine, I got to match shots with Jack Nicklaus. What did I know? I was just a Junior from Brockton, and he wasn't famous yet. I was playing on the Ohio State Scarlet Course in my Mass. foursome. We were joined by a couple of Ohio guys for the last four holes of our practice round. One of the Buckeyes was a blond boy, about six feet tall, who looked like a linebacker in Bermuda shorts. As I remember it, we were playing a par five hole, and I hit driver, three-wood, and a good nine-iron to the green. The blond kid needed no iron to the green. He hit a driver, then a three-wood to about 12 feet from the pin, then lipped out his putt for an eagle.

As I watched his fairway wood soar beyond my second shot by about 100 yards, I turned to one of my teammates and squeaked, "Who the heck is this guy?"

My equally awed teammate responded, "That's Jack Nicklaus. He can really play. And to make it worse, he knows this course cold."

Probably because he had that local knowledge, Jack Nicklaus edged me out...by 32 shots over 72 holes. With foresight that has become legendary, I predicted he'd never make it as a pro. I believe I called him a flash in the pan.

As one of my closest friends always reminds me, "Roly, don't you ever get tired of being right?"

High school heroics.

It was a weighty responsibility being the state champion. It was also a heavy load socially. Now, because of my new-found celebrity, I had no excuses for not being able to get a date. However, I was following in my brother Dick's footsteps, it seemed. I was definitely not considered a great French lover by the opposite sex, and neither had he been at this stage of post-adolescence. However, Dick was in college, and the dating drought continued to daunt him. It was a frightening prospect. What if it was genetic? A family trait? The lonely Lamontagnes, bachelor brothers forever!

High school was a high time for me. With the idea of diversifying my athletic career, I sought to extend my talents into the arena of basketball. To be completely honest, I also harbored the notion that making the team might also make me more dateable. Our Williams High School basketball team was league champion. Most of the basketball players played football as well. When the time for tryouts came, the two-sport guys were still finishing up the football season. That was my window of opportunity. I made it...as the twelfth man on a twelve-man team. I went into a game if we were 20 points ahead or behind, and then only for the last 30 seconds.

To illustrate my abilities without exaggerating, I was once inserted into a game with only 15 seconds remaining. In those last, fast 15 seconds, I managed to commit three personal fouls. I'm not sure if that's a world record, but it was definitely a record for my high school.

Perhaps my finest moment came in an away game at the gym of our arch-rival, Lawrence Central. Lawrence and Williams perennially played for the league championship. It was the second half. The game was close all the way. We had just gone up by a basket and had taken a time-out. The team ran off the floor to huddle around Coach John Bain. I didn't join the huddle, staying in my accustomed seat at the far end of the bench. I didn't bother because I knew I wasn't going in.

Suddenly, Coach Bain bellowed: "Lamontagne, get down here!"

Holy mackerel! The call. It had come. I was needed by my team in the most important game of the year. I got up and started toward the coach, dropping my warm-up pants and pulling my warm-up jacket over my head as I went. This was before pull-away velcro closures and quick-strip warm-ups. Picture a skinny kid trying to run with his pants around his ankles and his pullover jacket half way over his head. I was a pitiful sight, but nothing could stop me; I had been summoned to save the game for Williams High.

I arrived at the huddle breathless and still struggling to de-pants myself. All eyes were on me as I looked eagerly to Coach Bain for instructions. The coach riveted me with his stare. Then he said,

"Lamontagne, give Moynihan your shoe laces. He broke his."

"Oh, God", I thought, "why are you doing this to me?" I gave John Moynihan my laces, and he won the game for us. John and I had been close friends, but after the laces, things were never the same. Although indirectly I helped win the championship, I don't think I ever had a more humiliating experience. Not in public, at least. Incidentally, the episode did nothing to help my dating life. In fact, several cheerleaders asked me very loudly and publicly if I wanted to carry their shoelaces for them between classes.

I finally did get a date, the first of my life, late that winter. The girl was cute, attentive, and fortunately not a basketball fan. We went on a triple date...for her protection, not mine...and I remember worrying that one of my buddies might embarrass me by bringing up the shoelace story. They didn't, and the evening went well until they waited in the car while I escorted my date up the steep stairs to her front door. There must have been 20 steps, and they were all icy. I held her arm as we made our way carefully to the door. My suaveness was extremely apparent.

Came the moment of truth. I decided to go for it and kiss her goodnight. I'd seen guys do it in the movies, and it seemed like a good idea. It looked to me like she was puckered up and bright-eyed, expecting me to. However, as I leaned over to plant a cinema-inspired kiss and her eyelids flickered shut in anticipation, my feet went out from under me. Being a trained athlete, I managed to fall facing the street and bounced butt-first on all 20 of those icy steps.

My pals and their dates got out of the car and gave me a standing ovation. It was one of those times when growing up turned out to be extremely painful.

When golf season arrived, it came not a moment too soon to save my self-esteem. I was one of the team captains. High school golf in New England is decidedly different than it is down South or in California.

The Williams High golf squad was comprised of my co-captain, John "Laces" Moynihan, several seniors, and a hockey player named Billy Hinckley. The seniors included twin brothers who were truly tough; they won many matches simply because they were so menacing that it intimidated the opposition.

The other senior was a fancy dan named Jimmy Killory. It so happened that, on senior prom night, we had a match with another high school. Jimmy had his hair washed, cut, and coiffed for the big dance. He had lots of hair, set and gelled perfectly in the style of Buddy Holly. In fact, it was set so perfectly and it was so important to him that he declined to hit a critical bunker shot during the match. He refused to take the chance that sand would get into his hair. He forfeited the hole rather than injure his Holly hair-do.

The golf coach was a math teacher who wasn't much of a player. In fact, his basic coordination was highly questionable. I remember one incident during a match early in the spring when the coach, wearing a topcoat, was standing next to a small lake on the course. Our foursome teed off from an elevated tee. My partner, Billy Hinckley, hooked his tee shot into the water near the coach. We could see the ball go into the hazard. Our coach stood on the edge of the hazard by the red stakes and pointed to the spot where the ball had gone in. Steady as a rock during the entire time we walked toward him, the coach held that pointing position. As we neared him, he started to lean a little, still in the pose. Then, in slow motion, like the Leaning Tower of Pisa, he fell in. Our foursome fell down with laughter. I can still remember almost wetting my pants at the sight of our coach in his topcoat climbing out of the lake.

Summers during high school were wonderful periods in my life. I had a variety of summer jobs, working as a cook, then putting in curb stones, and finally cleaning out large industrial furnaces. When you are so covered with soot from the job that your own family doesn't recognize you, it's time to consider what you'll ultimately do for a living. That job made me make up my mind that I definitely wanted to go to college and that I absolutely wanted to do something clean for a living. Being a soot miner was not one of my long-term career goals.

Those years were magical. They replay in my mind like a home movie. When I worked at Bob & Ken's Restaurant until two in the morning every day, it left little time for a social life. But it didn't matter; it was neat in other ways. All the kids came in for a burger or fried clams, so they all knew me. Even my older brother's friends said "Hi, Roly" when they came in. It was a great job for an extrovert. The recognition was flattering, but it didn't translate into many dates. It's tough to impress a girl when you smell like a french fry.

Kids from my high school drove thirty miles to sit at the counter while I did my wisecracking soda-jerk act. Bob & Ken's made me a minor celebrity with my schoolmates. Back at school, it proved politically powerful. I was elected President of the Student Body, went on TV to represent my school, and was selected Student of the Month by the local radio station. The nuns even came to like me, and they stopped comparing me to my brother. Thank you for that, Bob and Ken.

Thorny Lea...the right club at the right time.

That summer when I was 17, I left the Brockton Country Club and was thrust into a fairly wealthy, younger private-club environment. The members of the Thorny Lea Golf Club gave me an honorary Junior membership. They were a gregarious, faster-living group with a collection of golf champions. The first day I played there, it just plain scared the hell out of me. It was my fully submerged baptism into the fraternity of weird and funny guys of golf.

My initial experience had been in Mr. Bell's foursome when I was eight. One of the golfers in Mr. Bell's foursome was Timmy Todd. I'll never forget him because he was the first of the many funny characters I've met in golf. Timmy Todd was a former pro baseball player who had grown short and round. He used to say that he was a fine golfer for his weight class. As an eight-year-old, I didn't understand the humor, but I remember him fondly now and chuckle appreciatively.

At Thorny Lea, it seemed to me that everyone was a character. And they all had funny nicknames: the Claw, "Smiley" Ed Connell, the Toscas - "Senor" and his son, "Junior", Saigon Bill, the Maestro, Saboo, the Banana Brothers, and many more. And the club had some members who could really play. Smiley Connell and Junior Tosca were both former Massachusetts State Amateur Champions. Another member, Leon Bishop, was the brother of U.S. National Amateur finalist, Ted Bishop.

Herbert Warren Wind, the author of the Ben Hogan book, belonged to Thorny Lea, along with his father, Max Wind, a local industrialist. They were great people. One day in my senior year of high school, Max Wind summoned me to his shoe factory and told me, "Your dad is a nice man, so I'm giving you some money for college."

Flabbergasted at this generosity, I replied, "Thank you, but I'm not sure I'll be able to pay you back."

Mr. Wind said, "You don't have to pay me back. Instead, you do the same for some other deserving kid when you're able to." God bless Mr. Wind.

Thorny Lea was quite a club. It seemed to me a model of democracy and tolerance. The membership was about equally composed of Jewish and Gentile, and as far as I could see, everyone got along with everyone else.

The clubhouse had old-money style and grace with a bar that perpetually offered a huge slab of cheddar cheese surrounded by a million crackers. I was allowed in the bar, but I never was permitted an alcoholic drink. I reveled in sitting there with a Collins mixer made by the bartender, Harry Black, who had been there since before the Revolutionary War. What a treat for a teenaged kid like me to sit and listen to the back-and-forth banter of the businessmen-golfers, their stories, the jokes, the humorous lies, and the laughter. And I never witnessed an untoward moment in that bar. Old Harry wouldn't have it.

The card games around the big, round tables were hilarious. Chips flew in all directions, the kidding was magical, and I was front-row audience to all the antics. God, it was great, funny stuff. A boy couldn't have a sweeter deal.

Brockton was the home of World Heavyweight Champion Rocky Marciano, and this was his era. Occasionally, he came to the club with his entourage of marginally sane followers. It was commonplace to walk into the men's locker room and find a few of Rocky's adherents shadow-boxing with the metal lockers. Those old lockers sure could take a punch.

The golf pro, Bill Shields, was at least 80 years old. He had an Irish brogue so thick you could cut it with a knife. Despite his age, there was never a thought of replacing him; I don't know why. You didn't mess with Old Man Shields, I do know that. He'd race his black 1955 four-door Ford around the golf course to make sure none of the caddies were out hunting for balls. Those were his golf balls, by damn! He was so tight that when he smiled his toes curled upward.

At Thorny Lea when I was 17, I got my first hole-in-one. It was early on a Sunday morning, when Junior members were not supposed to be on the golf course. My seven-iron on the 140-yard ninth hole went in the cup. I was more than a little excited. Expecting the high school band to greet me with "Hail to the

Chief", I ran to the pro shop to report my accomplishment and share my elation. That was a mistake. Old Man Shields stared stonily at me, then reminded me that I was a Junior member. Furthermore, I was banned from the golf course for one month for illegally playing on Sunday morning. That took the ho-ho out of my first hole-in-one.

What a great club it was, all in all! The members were a terrific bunch of guys. They treated me wonderfully well, let me get away with a lot, even let me make modest bets with them. But none of them would let me have a beer or a drink because they respected my dad and watched out for my best interests.

I got mad and walked off the course once in a fit of adolescent anger. The next week when I showed up to play in our regular match, my spot was taken. I was crushed. Senor Tosca told me, "If you want to play with the men, then act like a man." The following week, my spot was waiting for me. I learned my lesson and never stormed off the course again. Thank you, Senor.

The members knew that I was struggling with finances as a freshman in college. Before my sophomore year, they held a Roly Lamontagne Day and presented me with money and some terrific new clothes for college. Pretty nice stuff from a lot of kind, wonderful people who only wanted to help me. Just a bunch of golfers doing a good thing. Pretty nice stuff. Golf makes friends. You better believe it.

Years later, when I got out of the service, I came back to Thorny Lea. I was on my way from California to Florida for the

PGA Qualifying School with a stopover back in Massachusetts to visit my folks. At the club, it was like old home week. I had lunch with the whole gang, and about twenty of us decided to play a round for old times' sake.

One of the newer members, a Jewish doctor, had become part of the "rat pack" and joined us for this gala match. I hadn't known him before, and he had trouble pronouncing my name. However, the observant doctor did notice that I carried a rusty one-iron in my bag, and this apparently impressed him. He might have had trouble with his pronunciation, but there was nothing wrong with his eyes. As we set up the teams, I heard the doctor shout, "I'll take LaMoynihan with the one-iron!"

Yup, "La Moynihan!" By total coincidence, he called me by the name of the sunuvagun who had appropriated my shoe laces in the championship basketball game. My darkest moment come back to haunt me. It crossed my mind that one of my old friends might have put him up to a Freudian dig. Not so. To the doctor, "Lamontagne" translated to "La Moynihan." Never the less, it caught me off-balance.

Needless to say, my one-iron didn't perform up to par that day. Neither did what was above the handle. My less-than-inspired play prompted the good doctor to ask, "What qualifying school are you going to?", then, "Can you come back to your old job?"

"Not really," I replied. "I was an Air Force bombardier."

"Well, maybe you can start another war," the doctor said. He smiled knowingly, as if he had just finished examining me. I never found out what his specialty was, but I'm convinced the doctor must have been a proctologist.

A champion Dad and winning family.

Throughout every stage of my life, my family has been the greatest factor and support. And my father has been the most important influence in my life. When I was a little kid, he was the one hitting fly balls to my older brother Dick and me in the back yard. Dad did it despite a permanently bent right arm that had been broken and poorly reset. Harry Lamontagne worked in the Brockton Fire Department, a hard-working man with little time for himself. He always put his family first; I guess that's where I learned the importance of it.

When he got tickets to a ballgame, the best seats went to my brother and me, and Dad took what was left. Once, when he was invited by his firemen friends to go to a Red Sox - Yankees game at Fenway, he went without Dick and me for the first time. I whined and demanded to know why we couldn't go, until my brother ordered me to knock it off or he'd whack me one. Later, Dick tried to explain to me that Dad had the right to do things without us. I had a hard time grasping that. The fact that I couldn't understand it was a testament to his selflessness.

Whenever we played ball, he'd be up in the grandstand watching our Little League games. After each game, we'd go over the way we'd played. Dad would say, "Let's have some constructive criticism on the game." He knew his baseball, and the criticism was always positive and gentle. Then we'd go get an ice cream cone.

Dad and our younger sister Connie had a special father-daughter relationship that didn't have much to do with sports. He was highly focused on her feelings and her wellbeing. In response, Connie was the most responsible and best behaved of us kids. Dick and I called her "Glom" and gave her a lot of guff, but she handled it and us well. Right after Connie turned sixteen and got her license, she backed out of the garage and knocked a ladder over, denting and scratching the roof of the family car. It was the first big boo-boo of her life. She was inconsolable. Hoping to soften the shock for Connie, I called Dad at the Brockton Fire Department to let him know what had happened.

"Is everybody okay?" That was always his first thought.

"Yeah, but Connie is really upset," I replied.

"For God's sake," Dad exclaimed, "you and your brother have totaled two cars! Tell her she hasn't even put a dent in your record!" That was my dad.

A while before that, I'd had a head-on collision with a drunk driver and destroyed our new car. Frankly, if the other driver hadn't been blotto, I'd have been completely at fault. Relieved that I hadn't been hurt, my dad called the insurance agent and told him, "Do what you've got to do. I don't even want to look at it." Dad never blamed us for being kids or chastised us for the accidents of adolescence. He and Mom had raised us to be good, responsible kids, and we were. And he believed in us; that was the key.

Growing up, we always had only one car. That was limiting, with three kids and Mom, all going in different directions. Here, too, Dad was selfless. Every day, he walked three miles to work each way, and that included days with snowstorms, rain, and whatever. We kids managed to get around quite well. We had bicycles and rides and young legs. Now, when I think of my father walking to work and home every day, I marvel at his devotion and determination. It was a different world then, and he was quite a guy.

Later in life, when we were on our own, he got to drive his own car. And he drove until his death at 96. When I asked my brother how Dad was doing with the driving at his advanced age, Dick told me, "He hits what's not moving and chases it if it does move." Dad's impaired braking reflexes had moved the wall in Dick's garage back a few inches. A few inches of payback. What goes around comes around.

When I started to play golf, he was my most ardent supporter. He had dabbled with the game until he married my Mom. In fact, those hickory-shafted clubs I started with had been his. He gave me that "guaranteed hand-forged" set of MacGregor clubs, "made in Dayton, Ohio". It didn't matter that the set only lasted a year or two. So what if the hickory shafts shattered on cold Massachusetts days? They were undoubtedly the best hand-me-down present I ever got since they helped to shape my life.

Being the practical man that he was, Dad saw to it that we earned our own ways and learned the value of a buck. Early on, I earned my greens fees as a caddy, paper boy, and soda-jerk.

Later, in my teens, I had night jobs at restaurants so I could play golf during the days. We kids all understood that working was mandatory. The Lamontagnes always paid their bills, but usually there wasn't much left over.

As I progressed in golf, Dad became my mentor. While I began to gain some recognition for my abilities and got more attention in the newspapers, he guarded and guided my morals and priorities. He kept me from getting a big head and taught me what was really important in life. And he did it unobtrusively, always with kindness. To keep my brother, sister and me grounded in reality, he never overdid the praise, but we knew that he bragged about us proudly to his friends and co-workers.

When I got older and moved away, Dad wrote me the best letters. He had a knack for communicating heartfelt messages and for describing family news and local events in his own inimitable way. His letters were always sincere and enjoyable, reflecting Dad's own personality. It was a treat to get a letter specially addressed with a calligrapher's care, usually with a $10 bill enclosed; and I knew he went without something for himself to be able to send that money.

Everything in my life hasn't always been laughs and golf and sunshine. I want to get across the bad and the low times, too. I firmly believe they make the good times better and more meaningful. And I've learned that everything stems from everything else, good and bad. As when I finally received the call from Dick that I dreaded.

"Dad's had a stroke. You'd better grab a plane and come back here."

My father had fallen down in Dick's home, where Dad lived his last years. He'd tried repeatedly to get up and had bounced off the furniture in his bedroom, so he looked like somebody had beaten him up. By the time I got there, he was in the hospital. The diagnosis was that he had an inoperable brain tumor and, at 96, was nearing the end. He rallied briefly, and when I returned some weeks later, Dad was in the same rest home as my Mother. Mom had long been fully incapacitated by Alzheimer's, and Dad had visited her there for years. The disease had reduced her to a disoriented, little old lady who spent her days in a wheelchair. Dad had requested to be transferred there because it was his duty to be with his wife and take care of her. It was his code, "to take care of her forever."

Dad was dying; he knew he was dying; and he said to me, "Roly don't be angry with me, but I can't do this chemotherapy thing and the radiology because it makes me too sick. I'm 96, I've had a great life, and now it's my time."

However he wanted it was good with me. When I reached over and put my arms around him to pull him up and make him more comfortable, I was struck by how thin and frail he had become. We spent my entire last week with him talking about his life and the family and us as kids. That conversation didn't always make sense, but it was one of the most meaningful of my life.

When he wanted to talk, I sat on the edge of the bed and listened. He was my hero. What a life! Born before the Twentieth Century during an age of horseless carriages, he'd lived through the Wright Brothers' first flight and seen Neil Armstrong step on the moon. He had lived through two World Wars and witnessed the development of radio, television, and most of our technology. But mostly he talked about his "three great kids."

"I'll die a very lucky man," he said.

I just squeezed his hand; I couldn't talk.

Finally and mercifully, shortly after he died, my Mom passed away. I like to think that somehow she knew her life's companion wouldn't be able to visit her anymore.

When I have a problem or a predicament, there are times to this day when I find myself wondering what my Dad would do in my place. Much more than those hickory-shafted clubs, he shaped me. I don't think he ever broke 100 on the golf course, but when it came to life and his family, he was a scratch player.

Mom was a great mother and a perfect match for Dad. When she was younger, she was a tomboy and an excellent athlete. She was French Canadian, and she really was one of the boys. She hit like a guy and pitched like a guy. When I was in Little League, I would frequently ask her to warm me up. I was the catcher on the team. Despite the mitt and the sponge I used to cushion the catches, my hand would be bruised when she got done.

We called her "Ma", and she hated our sheep-like pronunciation of the word. If you got crossways with her, she chased you and thumped you like a man. All hell broke loose when she lost her Canuck temper.

She was extremely religious, having spent four years in the convent, studying to become a nun. I believe that had something to do with my dating disorientation. We went to church every Sunday and Catholic holy day; we said our prayers every night; and we knew that God ruled.

Mom had a bizarre, silent sense of humor. You had to know her to realize it. She used to sit in front of our black-and-white television set, watching Jackie Gleason or whatever, while she silently laughed. I have a memory image of this little woman totally appreciating the worst pratfalls in utter silence. Only her eyes and her smile gave away her internal glee.

I have seen my mother crack up with laughter. On a trip to San Francisco when my parents were old, Bev and I were walking and entertaining Mom and Dad. In later life, Dad was a real shutterbug and took photos of everything that stood still long enough. As we strolled through Chinatown, he was preoccupied with loading film into his camera and walked into a street light pole. I can still see it: the little 80-year-old man going full-force into the towering aluminum pole; the impact makes a sound like gong; fedora turned sideways, he bounces backward but doesn't miss a step.

Mom heard the gong and watched her husband ricochet off the pole. As Dad straightened his chapeau and checked himself for injuries, the film dropped out of the camera. Mom started laughing uncontrollably. While her laughter continued unabated, Dad looked at me with an embarrassed smile and kept walking. It took Mom two whole minutes to stop laughing and re-engage her walking gears.

She loved us all, and she fixed our hurts and hard times. Later in life, Alzheimer's robbed her of her sense of humor and joy in living. As with my Dad, I couldn't have asked for a better mother.

My older brother, Dick, was Mom's favorite. He did the right things while I was always the one who went a different way. He had chosen Holy Cross and majored in Greek and Latin. That was way too tough for me, and besides, Holy Cross was a college for men only. There were no coeds. Holy Cross had everything I didn't want.

He was a doer, but Dick wasn't much of a dater. A story my brother told me illustrated his frustrations with dating in college. One weekend, Dick and his roommate George decided to drive to a mixer with a women's college in Manhattan. It was purely a social gathering, with girls but without liquor. As my brother put it, "Beauty with a ban on booze. Shows how desperate we were."

At the start of the journey down the Mass. Pike, a student was hitchhiking before the toll booth. They decided to give the poor soul a ride, stopped, rolled down the car window, and yelled, "New York?"

The hitchhiker nodded okay, climbed into the back seat, and mumbled just enough to indicate that he was a little tipsy. He soon fell asleep.

The drive was uneventful until they unluckily caught the attention of a Massachusetts State Trooper, who pulled them over for speeding. The trooper was huge, about six and a half feet tall and weighing about 260 or more; not the type to be trifled with. He walked up to the driver's window, pad in hand, and asked, "Where's the fire, boys?"

"Well, sir, we're on our way to a mixer at a girls' college because we go to Holy Cross, a boys' college, and we haven't seen any women for one whole semester...and you know, sir...."

With that, the bon vivant in the back seat woke up and mumbled, "Whaz goin' on?"

The trooper shined his light in the red eyes of the back-seat passenger and growled, "Who are you?"

The passenger answered, "Officer, this silver bullet will explain everything."

Oh, God, it was the Lone Ranger, just when you needed him most. Paralyzing fear gripped my brother and his roommate.

They had visions of being dragged into a cell.

The behemoth trooper turned his face, trying to stifle his laughter, and said, "Boys, get out of here, and do it within the speed limit. Everyone needs a date once in a while, and you seem to need one more than most. You don't need a ticket, and I certainly don't need a silver bullet."

They went gratefully on their way, dropped the Lone Hitchhiker in the City, and went to the mixer. Appropriately, it was a bust.

I would have loved to go to college at Holy Cross like my brother, but the academics and the snow were against my nature. I decided that my college career would take place in a warmer, easier climate.

Dick was always the older brother I looked up to, but I never could tell him that. He had been held up to me by the nuns at Sacred Heart Grammar School as the ideal I should be like, and I resented it. When I came in from recess with a bloody nose, the good sisters commented, "Why can't you be more like your brother, Richard?"

We lived in a pretty tough neighborhood. Even though we might be personally at odds, Dick always stuck up for me and acted as my defender. He was always bigger than I was, and the brotherly fights between us were mostly hit-and-run on my part. I was brave and quick, but not suicidal.

As I became more frivolous in high school, Dick became more serious. He was a smart guy, got good grades, and ended up at Holy Cross with a NROTC scholarship. Then he went into the Navy as an officer. He was a tough act to follow. College actually spelled the end of our close relationship. Later, he stayed in the East, and I ended up in California. We've gone in different directions, but we're still the two brothers who scrapped in the back yard in Brockton. And he's still my big brother.

My sister, Connie, was the little lady who completed the family. In every family, God puts someone special, someone sweet. Connie was the chosen Lamontagne. She was the baby, the quiet girl, the introspective woman. From the beginning, she was special.

When she was an infant, I batted a baseball through a bedroom window during a backyard game. It ended up in her crib. She didn't cry; she just stared at the baseball. She already knew better than to squeal on her brother.

Connie was always our pal and our patsy. She never fought with us, and she never caused us any grief. She was smarter than we were. Dick and I had a dilemma because Connie wasn't a typical snotty little sister. What do you do with a little girl who is related to you and is so nice?

One thing was for sure. Nobody messed with our sister. She grew into a pretty, intellectual, mellow girl who was very popular. A terrific student, she proved to her brothers that you don't have to be a jock to get a college scholarship, and she went on to get her Master's degree. Brains over brawn; that describes her relationship with me.

My sister possessed the considerate kindness of my father and the best qualities of my mother. Many times, as I wobbled through various stages of my life with personal problems, she sent me a loving card or note at precisely the right moment. It's as if she has extra-sensory perception that tells her when to uplift her bothered brother.

She's gotten what she deserved, the best; married to a great guy and has five fine kids. I truly regret that we live 3,000 miles apart. If they gave out trophies for superb sisters, Connie would have won the prize permanently.

That's the entire Lamontagne family. I'm proud that I belong to them and I owe them my love and appreciation for the best things in life.

Getting to the green.

My journey in golf took me slowly toward the PGA Qualifying School. But life is a twisty, turny thing, and a lot happened along the way.

I went to college at Rollins in Winterpark, Florida, where I played on the golf team and thoroughly enjoyed college life, and then went into the U.S. Air Force for six years. I can summarize those years with a brief description of my introduction to Rollins and my exit from the Air Force.

At Rollins, the front entrance was flanked by two low brick walls. The sun was shining. The flowers were blooming. And gorgeous girls in bathing suits were sunning themselves on the walls. It was perfect. I knew immediately I had chosen the correct college for me.

On June 28, 1968, after six years in the United States Air Force, I went through the gates of Mather Air Force Base in California just as a bunch of B52 bombers took off. I turned for one last look and thought of all the kids I had helped train and all the friends I had lost in Vietnam. I felt guilty that I had never seen combat. Although I lived near Mather for many years after, I rarely visited the base.

So there I was: Mr. Lamontagne, college-educated, former officer, freshly civilian again, and 28+ years in the making. Kind of old for a rookie golf pro.

I declared as a professional and applied to the Northern California PGA for Players School, which was held in Florida. Because of my amateur record, I was one of the few to be selected. Out of more than 800 professionals who petitioned to attend the PGA Players School, only about 100 were accepted. Of the 100, only 30 earned their permit. I finished sixteenth in the qualifying.

By the way, it wasn't really a school; that was just a nice way of describing this preliminary professional pressure-cooker. It was an eight-day, eight-round, 144-hole tournament with some classes on the side...and it was absolutely the most pressure-packed event I've ever been privileged to play in. If you qualified, you went on the tour; if you didn't qualify, you went on to find a real job in the real world.

Class instruction was provided by the PGA staff. They taught us that profanity and pitching clubs or caddies into the lake were considered bad manners and would be fined. They instructed us to be careful in our choice of attorneys, warning us to avoid lawyers who began, "Pssst, have I got a deal for you!" Classes and practice rounds took the better part of the first week. The schooling aspect was secondary. In reality, the whole thing was more like golf's version of the Indianapolis 100 with eager pros waiting to "start their engines."

During one of my first practice rounds, I met Malcolm Gregson, a great guy from Great Britain and a multi-winner on the European Tour. Malcolm was an excellent golfer, a British Ryder Cupper, a class act, and a character. For some reason, we hit it off and became friends right away.

For a subsequent practice round, Malcolm and I were paired with another player who shall remain nameless because he turned out to be a real jerk. Nameless came over and introduced himself, proclaiming that he was the current Washington State Open Champion. He knew Malcolm to be the number two player on the British Order of Merit and asked me who in the world I was.

With savvy accumulated though ten years of college and military service, I knew that Mr. Washington Open Champ would not be impressed by my credentials. Among my many titles, the most recent was Roseville City Champion, population 5,000. So, with appropriate seriousness, I introduced myself as the reigning "Shingle Springs Driving Champion."

He snorted, "What and where the hell is that?"

"Shingle Springs is between Latrobe and Rescue," I responded. "It's one of the great tests of driving ability in the country."

Malcolm knew I was putting the guy on and didn't say a word. He just stood on the first tee with an amused smile on his face. We teed off. Malcolm crushed one down the middle of the fairway. Nameless nailed one just as pure that ended up next to Malcolm. Not to be outdone, the Shingle Springs Driving Champion reached back and fired a vicious snap hook into a palm tree 135 yards down the left side of the fairway.

Nameless chuckled and remarked, "Obviously not your best, Mr. Driving Champion."

"Bullshit it wasn't," I replied emphatically. "That's how much you know. The first hole at Shingle Springs is a short dog-leg left."

Malcolm cracked up. "That was bloody good!" We became buddies forever.

The tournament finally began. Anyone who shot even par, 288 for four rounds, automatically received their card. Malcolm and the current NCAA Champ were the only two who qualified that way. The rest of us qualified the old-fashioned way; we earned it by playing all 144 grueling holes. That included Jim Jamieson, Ed Sneed, Jerry Heard, and myself. The Washington State Open Champion failed to qualify.

The days went by quickly and slowly at the same time. Each morning, we shrugged off the misfortunes of the day before and restarted our engines. We were all beginning to show the effects of more pressure than any of us had experienced before in our golfing careers.

Every night, some of us would walk on the beach, trying to relax. I occupied myself by throwing stones at the schools of mullet that swam along the shore. I became so proficient that Malcolm named me "the Mullet Stoning Champion of Shingle Springs."

Many of these guys were at the school for their second, third or fourth tries. There were no mini or alternative tours back in those days, only a few foreign tours. If you could afford it, you could possibly play out of the country, but everyone wanted to play the PGA Tour. The pressure began to take its toll on some of the players.

On the eighth and final day, I was paired with Jim Jamieson, a great player who, for whatever reason, was in his third attempt to get his card. According to Jim, this was his final attempt. He played lights-out for seventeen holes and could have qualified with a ten on the last hole, so he was in. Needless to say, he was one happy golf professional.

My fate was still undecided, and I was grinding. I needed a four. Jim hit a great drive. I skied my drive. I hit next, a one-iron on the green, but a long way from the pin. Jamieson put it up there close. I trudged down the eighteenth fairway with my chances in the hands of the golf gods, knowing I was teetering on the brink. I looked up when I heard Jim yahooing and turned to see him throw his club high into the air. More yahoos! With each yell, he launched another club into the sky. The celebratory club throwing caught the eye of Pete Sesso, PGA Tour official, who came flying down the fairway in his official's cart.

Red-faced, Sesso shouted at Jamieson, "You throw one more club and it's a hundred dollar fine!"

Jamieson was so elated he couldn't be contained. "I've only got four clubs left," he shouted back. "I'll give you $500, and you can keep the change!" With that, the four clubs went airborne. Pete Sesso smiled disgustedly, turned and drove away.

I two-putted from about 90 feet. My first putt was within two feet. I tapped it in. I was sweating in places where I had never sweated before, but I was finished. My tank was empty, but I'd done it.

I had qualified. Once again, I was ready for the next door to open, and it couldn't open soon enough to suit me. I had $77 to my name. My only other money was in a checking account I couldn't use unless I qualified. Just to make it more precarious, I was 2,400 miles from home and my credit cards were already maxed out. Looking back, I ask myself if I was ever that young and confident to put myself at such risk. My answer is 'I'd do it again', and I wish I could.

Tiger Woods got 47 million dollars up front when he became a pro. Just to give an idea how different things were in my day, my only help came from the Spalding Company. I received two dozen balls from Spalding. I used the 1s in the first round and the 8s in the eighth round of Players School. I still have the Spalding Dot 8 from that final qualifying hole. Would I sell it for $47 million? Well, maybe.

On the Tour.

Whenever I get too wound up in the game, I think of a moment narrated by the famed announcer and PGA Champion, Ken Venturi, who was describing the deciding holes of a tournament on television in the 1990s. A rookie...whose name I've long since forgotten...stood on the eighteenth fairway, needing a career shot to the distant green. The young man had been through four days of unimaginable pressure, playing in swirling winds, contending with the rigors and hazards of the difficult course. Not used to being among the leaders, his nerves were raw, his shirt was soaked, and his palms were wet with perspiration.

The flag was on the edge of a tiered green beside a huge lake. To make matters worse, the hole position was on a peninsula of the green surrounded by water. The slightest mishit would put his ball and his dream of victory into the lake. The rookie had to hit a controlled 2-iron fade 240 yards. His shot would have to come in perfectly on the left side of the green and move toward the flag that was set on the lowest tier. If he put it on the green, he still needed to two-putt to win the tournament. So many obstacles; so much pressure; so much riding on this one swing.

It was the shot that could change the course of his career. If he pulled it off, he'd be a bona fide PGA tour event winner, exempt from qualifying each week, no longer a Monday morning trunk-slammer. This shot literally meant everything to him. Unless you've been there, you can't imagine his thought process, the migraine focus inside his head, muscles doing the Macarena twitch. He had to be fighting the negative and disruptive thoughts that crowd the mind at a time like this.

Because I had competed briefly on the tour, I had a great appreciation of what the rookie was feeling. My own experiences made his moment even more dramatic, and I empathized as I watched and waited.

Venturi commented to his sidekick in the booth, "He's probably thinking he'll fade a 2-iron in there and let it feed down to the pin."

Yeah! Right, Kenny! That's exactly what the kid was thinking! But I've been there, and I don't think so!

Let me tell you what the rookie was probably thinking: "Oh, God, please don't let me make a fool of myself by scaling this baby into the water...and please don't let me wet my pants on national TV." At this point, the kid was way past Venturi's fading and feeding analysis.

The young man hit a bullet to the green, faded it perfectly, two-putted, and lived happily ever after. Everyone, including Venturi, was elated. I sat in front of the television with tears in my eyes. I felt as if I had been in that rookie's body. I had experienced his emotions, fears, and the final incredible rush of happiness that only victory can produce. It was a wonderful feeling, a rare and marvelous moment that captured all the allure and drama of competitive golf.

It didn't happen like that for me. My qualifying card, that little piece of prized paper, got me in but not up on any leader board. My PGA card permitted me to tee it up with the other rookie pros trying for the few open spots in the PGA tournaments. We were called "rabbits" or "trunk-slammers" because we gypsied across the country, carried all our equipment in the trunk, and showed up on Monday morning hoping to qualify for each tournament. There were a lot of us vying for four or five places each week.

It was life on the edge. Tee it up on Monday to qualify. If you didn't qualify, throw your clubs and suitcases into the trunk, slam it, and head for the next tournament stop. The big names arrived on Tuesday evening to play in the Wednesday Pro-Am. Most of the trunk-slammers had already left town. If you didn't qualify, there was not a lot of hobnobbing with the big boys. In fact, there were really two tours going on, and I was usually part of the one that played early in the week. It was a crazy, run-around life that made sense only to those who loved the game. It was made for me. I wouldn't trade that experience for $47 million; well, maybe.

My first event was the Haig & Haig Invitational. I had driven cross-country to California in five days to arrive on Sunday night, only to find out that I had been assigned a very early morning tee time. The qualifying site was the Costa Mesa Public Golf Course.

I had never seen it or even heard of it, but I was ready. I felt the sun was coming up that morning especially for me.

At 7:00 AM I was waiting with great anticipation on the first tee. Everyone else was loosening up on the practice tee. I was vibrating with excitement and wishing I'd brought a diaper. It was a good thing that I'd been well toilet-trained by my parents because I was fighting the urge to pee my pants.

My first tee shot on the tour was a thing of beauty, right down the middle. I stood and watched it proudly. It was perfect. I was euphoric. This was the moment you dreamed about while you were hitting 100,000 practice balls.

My second shot was only 140 yards to an easy green. Seven iron. No problem for Mr. Accuracy. Just put that picture-perfect swing on it and...Mayday! Mayday! I hit a shank. God, how embarrassing! I checked to make sure I hadn't hit one of my old hickory-shafted starter clubs by some horrible accident. My urge to pee dried up, along with all the fluids in my body.

I skulked through the rough to the adjoining fairway and surveyed the damage, trying to put my screw-up out of my mind. Sand wedge, don't fail me now. I hit it over the trees and slam-dunked my 20-foot par putt. Whew! Good save. The aircraft may have suffered a sudden flame-out, but, by Gawd, we brought her in safely for a near-perfect landing. The reclaimed par really got me going, and I started to play well.

My wife was standing behind the 9th green as I made the turn, and she asked me hesitantly, "How are you doing?"

"I only have five pars so far," I responded.

She looked a little downcast, but brightened and said, "That's okay, babe, you can do it." She started to say some more encouraging words, but I interrupted. I didn't have the heart to put her on.

"Yeah, five pars," I said happily, "but I also had four birdies!" She brightened considerably.

Damn! I was enjoying this. I even did a little showing off for my bride on the next hole. The 10th hole was a par-five, and I stuck it on in two for an easy birdie, my fifth birdie in ten holes. To make a long day short, I qualified. Right out of the box, first attempt, first success. I was on top of the world. This was great stuff.

The site of the tournament was actually the Mesa Verde Country Club. As I drove through the gates, I was stopped by a volunteer who informed me that the parking lot was reserved for the players. After I stammered, "I am a player!", the gentleman offered to park my car for me. I rode down into the lot with him and made conversation. As a matter of fact, I seized on the opportunity to talk because I was nervous. Actually, I was apprehensive of going to the players' sign-in tent. I hadn't figured out what to say if Arnie or Jack asked me to join them for a practice round.

My driver was a nice fellow, and the conversation calmed me. I was very concerned to relate well to my new golfing public. I asked him if he worked at the club. No, he was a member and had volunteered to help. "I work for a bank here in town," he said.

I wanted to put him at ease. He probably hadn't been been around that many sub-par touring professionals. So, in my best sub-par touring professional manner, I asked, "And what do you do at the bank?"

"I'm the president of it," he answered matter-of-factly.

Damn! This tour thing was beyond my imaginings. I didn't tell him that the bank president was parking a first-tournament rookie's car.

As it turned out, I had worried needlessly. I made it to the sign-in tent, and neither Nicklaus nor Palmer approached me. In fact, I never even saw either one at the sign-in tent; perhaps they had a different agenda than I did. I didn't know anyone, and I was a little jittery about how to arrange a practice round. Bob E. Smith, a pro from Sacramento, spied me and yelled, "Sign in, Frog, we're on the tee!" I fought back the urge to kiss Smitty on the lips; I was that glad to see him. His greeting erased my newcomer's uneasiness.

I survived the rigors of signing in, and we went to the first tee. Practice rounds were by threesome, and our third was a veteran touring pro from the Northwest named Bob McAllister. There I was...first tee...first tournament practice round. It was Monday, and I didn't have to put my stuff in the trunk. Everything was wonderful. Life was just a bowl of golf balls!

While we waited to hit, I roamed around the first tee, picking up white wooden tees. Unbroken tees were everywhere, just left there by the previous threesomes. They were like new, bright and shiny. I collected a handful and stuffed them in my bag, then knelt to pick up more. When I stood up, McAllister came over and put his arm around my shoulder. I was certain he was going to offer some veteran advice or encouragement because he had immediately taken a liking to me. He said quietly so no one else could hear, “Roly, don’t pick up the tees. You don’t need to stockpile; they give you all the tees you want out here.”

Roly, the tee-taker. Roly, the rookie. Thanks for telling me quietly, Bob...so no one else could hear what a new-boy I was.

As fate would have it, in my initial round I was paired with my pal, Malcolm Gregson, and Bobby Cox, a pro from Canada. A Brit, a Canadian, and Roly the Frog...sounds truly international, doesn’t it? But it didn’t help me much because I didn’t make the cut. Actually, I had to withdraw during the second round because of a back muscle strain. And from that I learned a lesson.

My back problem was the result of sleeping in a bad bed in a cheap motel to save money. The bed was so bad it should have had a bio-hazard warning posted on the headboard. From that, I learned it’s not worth it to scrimp on essentials. No more cheap joints! A veteran tour pro confirmed that when he told me: “Eat hamburgers, and you’ll play like a hamburger.”

Next stop was the Olympic Club in San Francisco to play in the final Lucky Open. I slept in a good, sound bed and fired a 68 to qualify. So far, so good. Two tournaments, and I was two for two. My trunk remained unslammed.

This was my first event with folks I knew in the gallery. A

contingent of friends and people from Sacramento had come to see me play. I was nervous and shot a 76 the first day, followed by a 71 to miss the cut. Two for two on that, too, but I was learning valuable lessons.

During this tournament, Roly the Rookie learned about caddies. Because I was a trunk-slammer, I was issued a scrub caddie, and I paid for it...literally and figuratively. My scrub caddie asked for two days' pay up front. I gave it to him. On the second day, he was nowhere to be found. It got to tee-off time, and he still hadn't shown. The PGA Official directed me to tee off and carry my own bag, and he'd send out a regular caddie whose pro had withdrawn.

I hit a good tee shot, and by the time I reached it, a professional caddie was there. He showed up with an attitude, but he showed up. For my second shot, I hit a 7-iron about ten feet from the flag. We lined up the putt together, and he muttered, "Two inches left edge." I read it to be two inches right edge. Without saying anything, I chose my line and missed the putt by about five inches to the right. His read had been correct.

Sheepishly, I turned to the obviously disgusted caddie and mumbled, "Rookie mistake, huh?"

"Yeah," he growled, "and if you don't listen, you'll be a goddamned rookie for the rest of your life."

There was no misunderstanding that advice. I kept it in mind for the rest of my golf career. We worked well together for the rest of the round, but it was too little too late.

Hawaii was next. It was a little too far and a little too wet to drive there. I skipped it because I couldn't afford the airfare. Money was tight, and I was searching for backers.

Then came a tournament called the Cajun Classic, held in Lafayette, Louisiana. That was where my Northeastern middle-class sensibilities and my socioeconomic awareness received a severe jolt. It had to do with my caddie, a young African-American lad who immediately made himself my friend. We teamed up terrifically well and forged a great relationship. His name was James, and he was a real champ.

James and I made the cut. I say that "we made the cut" because tour caddies always say we when their player does something positive, but it's he when the player blows it out of bounds or three-putts.

We played well in the third round, and I wanted to show my appreciation for James's input. After the round, I gave him a putter and a wedge that I didn't need and offered him a ride home. He took me on an uncertain, circuitous trip to the poorest part of town to a very modest house. When I dropped him off, I asked him the best way to get back to the Howard Johnson Motel, where I was staying. I could see it across the bayou.

"You can't get there from here," James replied, and went into the house with the clubs I had given him. He wasn't a wiseguy and didn't deal in sarcasm, so it surprised me.

I didn't get it, but on the drive back, after reconstructing our conversations on the course, I believe I came to understand his answer. It derived from his poverty and his simple honesty. James only knew how to get to two places. He knew his way to school and he knew the way to work at the Oakbourne Country Club. To him at that point in his young life, the rest of the world simply didn't exist. He knew only what he knew, and that was that.

It made me realize the effects of poverty and color in a different world than that in which I had grown up. Isn't it amazing that it took me almost thirty years to realize the reality of this shocking, sad situation? I had grown up and gone through college and military service without seeing such inequality firsthand, only to be confronted by it because of my caddie at the Cajun Classic. This jolt to my awareness was heightened by my feeling of friendship for my new pal. I don't know what happened to James. I lost track of him, but I remember vividly that ride and his answer, "You can't get there from here." I hope he got there. He was a terrific kid and a great caddie.

The Cajun Classic was more than socio-economically enlightening; it was also kind to my budding career. I had played 72 holes and earned an automatic entry into the Los Angeles Open. That meant I didn't have to qualify. On Wednesday, feeling like a seasoned pro, I checked in at the players' tent. Wow, was I on my way or what? The players' tent! My starting time did not quite match up to my feeling of professional status. It was 6:30 AM on the tenth tee at Rancho Park.

At exactly 6:30, our tour official, Jack Tuthill, motioned at me and barked, "Lamontagne, you're up."

"You're kidding," I objected. "It's still dark!"

"Hit it!" Tuthill ordered. "When the ball comes down, the sun will be out."

In this unlikely setting, I witnessed my first miracle: I hit the ball, and while it was in the air, the sun came over the horizon. Since then, I've always stood in awe of Jack Tuthill.

The rest of the day was uneventful except for one misplay. I was teamed with Paul Bondeson and Rafe Botts. On a par-three near a hot dog concession, I shanked a strong 4-iron right into the tent. Buns flew and hot-dog lovers dove under the condiment table. I thought we might have to call an ambulance...for my playing partners. They were on the ground, laughing at me.

When he recovered enough to speak, Rafe remarked that I was definitely a "hot dog player."

Naturally, Roly the Rookie had to ask what that was. Rafe explained that I was that kind of player who, when he approached a green with a gallery surrounding it, inspired the entire gallery to leave to get a hot dog. It took me a long time to learn not to ask dumb questions. However, it didn't take long to be put in my place professionally; I missed the cut in L.A. and set off to qualify on Monday for the next trunk-slamming event.

Despite my limited success, times were getting tough. My money was running low. My concentration was more on finding some backers than on firing some birdies. My state of mind was not good for my game. But I kept going.

To the Kaiser Open at Silverado in Napa. It was a prestigious tournament in a beautiful setting. Monday morning qualifying took on a new twist for me when I was paired with an amateur named Billy DuHain. Billy was a professional hockey player, a forward for the Chicago Blackhawks. He had injured his knee and was rehabbing by a lot of walking and golf. Like so many other hockey players, he was a good golfer. There must be a natural correlation between the golf swing and swinging a stick while skating in balance. Anyway, I would call Billy a good stick in either sport.

Because I was an avid Boston Bruins fan, Billy and I had a lot to talk about. I noted his small stature and asked him what was the most frightening hockey brawl he'd ever been in. His story is worth the retelling. Unfortunately, it turned out to be the high point of my round that day.

The previous season, the Blackhawks were in a bench-clearing brawl with the Detroit Redwings. And the Redwings star was the legendary Gordie Howe, a big, slope-shouldered superman who weighed well over 200 pounds, all muscle. Billy, who weighed between 140 and 150 pounds, ended up with Gordie Howe. Gloves off, they held each other's arms. As Billy said, "Gordie's arms were as big as my thighs." Billy looked up into Howe's eyes and said nothing, but knew he was in for an ambulance ride. Howe looked down at Billy and said, "Okay, kid, we just dance. No swinging." According to Billy, he replied with something like: "Yes, sir, Mr. Howe." They dance-skated around the fracas until order was restored, and Howe took his hands off Billy's shoulder pads. Gordie tapped Billy lightly on the chin and said, "Ya did good, kid." before he skated away. Billy skated back to his bench and looked up, thanking God for sparing his life.

That added much-needed humor to my round, but the result wasn't funny. I didn't qualify. As I drove away from Silverado, I thought to myself: 'You better get going, Roly. Get some backing. Get your game together. Get yourself together. Otherwise, you're gone, rookie.'

The course of my life.

I went home to Sacramento to relieve the pressure of the road and hopefully to find a sponsor. The Bing Crosby at Pebble Beach was next, but my money was down to the leather in my wallet. Just when things were looking their bleakest, I received a call from a prominent Sacramento attorney. He told me he was interested in helping me, and could I come down to his office? This bordered on the miraculous. It ranked right up there with Jack Tuthill making the sun come up. Could I come to his office? Could I make a one-inch putt? I could have outrun the roadrunner to get there. My salvation was at hand.

I was in his office at 8:00 the next morning. We talked. My benefactor was a successful lawyer, an interesting, likeable man, and a golfer. He'd experienced hard times when he was young and knew what it meant to need a backer. We liked each other immediately. He wrote out a substantial check to me and signed the sponsor's contract that I had made sure to bring.

What a moment that was! While still in his office, I looked up, expecting dark clouds to part and a heavenly beam of light to penetrate the office ceiling and illuminate me. This man and his faith in me were exactly what I needed. And his financial backing. And not a moment too soon. Talk about your last-second saves and your gallows reprieves! It was all the sweeter because it came just when it seemed I was finished. That check was my ticket to the tour.

Look out, Nicklaus, Palmer, whoever. I was renewed and ready to do battle. The rest of the day, I showed the check to anyone who'd look at it and celebrated my good fortune.

The game plan was to deposit the check the next morning and head to Pebble for some practice time. During breakfast, before packing the car, I was reading the Sacramento newspaper. One headline jumped up and bit me. It read: PROMINENT ATTORNEY DIES. Suddenly I had a hard time breathing. My new sponsor had suffered a heart attack and passed away, all within 24 hours of signing my contract. I was devastated. I even hoped that the act of meeting me hadn't contributed to his heart attack. What was the right thing to do?

I talked it over with Bev, and we decided I should talk to his brother, also an attorney and his partner. I went back to that office with a heavy heart. The brother reviewed the legal aspects and informed me that the transaction was legitimate. However, while the money was mine to use, he told me that my sponsor had left a wife and three children and no life insurance. I heard his words as if I was in an echo chamber. His words sounded muffled and distant, but they were all too clear. So it was clear what I had to do. Feeling like I was made of lead, I produced the check and handed it over. He shook my hand and gave me a heartfelt pat on the back.

"Good luck, Roly, and I'm sorry."

That was the worst. Good bye, Roly was the real message. Good bye, time. Good bye, tour. Goodbye, dream. We went to Pebble. Spyglass was the qualifying site. The rest was just a blur. However, there is a memory I will carry forever from that day. I walked up the eighteenth fairway with my head down, knowing I hadn't qualified. As I approached the green, I glanced up and saw Bev and Michelle behind it, silhouetted against the magnificent backdrop. I had a hard time meeting their eyes. Bev saw my face and knew it was over. Michelle held her mother's hand, sensing something had gone wrong. It seemed to me at that instant that the world was leaving me behind.

After the tour, life seemed quiet and lusterless. I bounced around a bit, floundering to find myself, but eventually golf again provided opportunities. I became a club professional, first at a driving range, then at Hoffman Park Golf Club. At Hoffman, I came under the wing of Mike Macaluso, the head pro, and I learned a lot from Mike in the six months I was his assistant.

It was Mike who instructed me in proper customer service. When a nearby cocktail lounge was holding its annual golf outing at Hoffman, Mike asked me to refrain from announcing over the public address system: "Hear this, all you lushes: the next foursome is on the first tee." When I couldn't understand the problem with that, Mike forcefully ordered me to knock it off and shape up. We had that kind of a working agreement.

It was obvious to both of us that our agreement wasn't going to work, so we made a new agreement: I'd look for another job and he'd look for another assistant. We'd keep it civil and give each other time to do our thing comfortably.

That was the arrangement until one Saturday morning when I arrived at the club to open up at 5:00 AM. As I walked to the pro shop, I noticed that the lights were on and the door was open. My initial thought was that we were being burglarized. Stealthily, I sneaked up to the door. Perhaps cowardly would be a better way to put it. I had no intention of putting myself in harm's way for some golf equipment.

I peeked in to spy a young man, clean-cut and confused, standing behind the counter. He was not armed. Calling up all the bravery I could muster, I leaped through the doorway and demanded, "Who are you and what are you doing here?"

The young man stared at me in stunned surprise and squeaked, "I'm the new assistant pro. Who are you?"

"I think I'm the old pro," I replied with increasing understanding. He smiled sheepishly, obviously embarrassed that we were meeting this way. "Where the hell is Macaluso?" I asked.

"He's on his way in," my replacement replied.

Thinking it over during the awkward silence that followed, I could feel my blood pressure rising. I thought Mike and I had a deal. I had agreed to give him a week's notice, and he was supposed to do the same for me.

Well, it wasn't the new guy's fault, so I introduced myself and helped him get the pro shop ready for business. I showed him how to open the safe; he didn't know the combination. I demonstrated how to use the sheet, run the cash register, and turn the microphone on.

Mike Macaluso showed up, and I could feel myself getting hot. I was so angry I could hardly talk, but I started to say something that probably would have inflamed the situation. Before I could get it out, Mike ordered me to "calm down, sit down, and listen." I did. Mike handed me a check and said, "Here's two weeks' pay. Now you can look for work, and you don't have to worry about this place. Is that fair?"

I had to agree that it was more than fair. Our deal was only for one week, and I'd been searching for a new job in the evenings after I finished work. This freed me up to look full-time. It turned out that Mike Macaluso was a good guy. We parted company, but ended up friends. Once again, I was treated better than I probably deserved.

Out of dire necessity, I found my next position in golf. And while it seemed dire at first glance, it turned out to be a great job and a great place. It was at Swallow's Nest, a nine-hole course on 40 acres, a former peach farm converted into a culture shock. I was hired to be the Head Professional. I still don't know whether that was a step up or down for me. The first hole was 97 yards long. Three par-fours were each only about 300 yards in length, but each had its own irrigation lake.

It was another world. When I arrived, I discovered that the

course tractor was actually a converted aircraft tow motor. Lucky thing I'd been in the Air Force. Too bad the thing was mired knee-deep in a muddy fairway. Worse still that it didn't work. The only equipment that worked at Swallow's Nest was the horse tied up in the back. And the horse couldn't be used to mow the greens. This was to be my new home. I fit right in. My transition from the PGA Tour was complete.

As my first official act, I insisted that the tow motor be relegated to the junk heap and that we purchase a proper tractor and suitable equipment to keep up the course. We obtained a "like new" used Jacobsen Tractor. The seller assured us that it had been fixed up and tuned for the rigors of topography at Swallow's Nest.

I inherited a crazy crew and a maintenance guy named Otto, a young man with enormous physical strength. Demonstrating the expertise and take-charge attitude of the entire crew, Otto decided to fine tune the tractor for optimum performance. According to the manual, the tractor's fuel jets should be adjusted only by hand-tightening. Otto snapped off the first fuel jet he tightened by hand. Oops! That taught me not to shake hands with Otto and to watch him carefully around the machinery.

Although my contract said nothing about "jack of all trades", I became the golf professional, course manager, and greens superintendent...out of dire necessity...all in a very short time. Thus, I became known as the Head Swallow, a title that seemed to fit my all-around status.

At the Nest, when we top-dressed the greens, it was accomplished in a less sophisticated manner than was employed at Augusta or Pebble Beach...or perhaps anywhere else, including Baghdad. We top-dressed with shovels from a Cushman maintenance cart and finished off with a flat asphalt rake. It was backbreaking work. One day, in my multi-faceted role as greens superintendent, I sent my entire gang out to top-dress all nine holes in 12 hours. It was a killer task, and it made me about as beloved by the crew as a flash flood in a crowded men's room.

Hard work appeals to me; I could watch it for hours; but even for me, this was too much. Sensing that I might not win the popularity contest that day, I decided to show that I was one of the guys by joining in the work. So I jumped on the Jacobsen to mow the fairways while the crew was doing the greens. It was a way to convince them that I wasn't just another elitist management clown. In the course of mowing, whenever I approached the crew on the greens, they emphatically ignored me. Basically, I was being shunned. I could have been burned up, but I wasn't. Because I am the type of dependent person who needs to be loved, I felt bad. Every time I came near them with the mower, they tuned me out.

Finally, on a pass down the longest fairway, everyone in the crew stared at me with obvious caring concern and began to wave. I can't tell you how good it made me feel to know how they really felt about me. They liked me. No, they loved me. What a great bunch of guys. I blissfully waved back, and they waved back at me with even more animation. Some were smiling, some were laughing. Everyone was into the moment.

Otto ran down the fairway to meet me. He was yelling something. I throttled back and leaned forward to hear what he was hollering about.

"Shut it down! Turn the tractor off! The engine is on fire!"

After we put the flames out, I showed the crew my appreciation by joining the top-dressing. I got more snickers and sarcastic smiles than conversation. They still shunned me for the rest of the day, but pitching in made me feel better. I could have been burned up, but I wasn't.

As Head Swallow, I became fairly adept at all the tasks necessary to maintain a golf course: installing drains, cutting greens, gang-mowing fairways. I never got good at top-dressing, probably because I totally avoided it after my back healed. And I almost ordered a fireproof suit like the race drivers wear, but I would have looked ridiculous mowing the fairways in it. Gradually, I got back in the crew's good graces, and they came to fully realize the extent of my abilities.

Like most golf professionals, one of my primary responsibilities was to give lessons. Unfortunately at Swallow's Nest, I primarily gave lessons to the legally blind, the lame, and the uncoordinated. My roster of lesson-takers was mainly made up of ungifted golfers who had been shunned by the more established golf teachers in the area. Those pros didn't have the time or vision or patience to put up with pathetic pupils on the practice range. Many of my students were depressed over their lack of game and one step away from slashing their wrists. However, this collective suicidal tendency was never a problem. Judging by their swings, they were incapable of slashing; judging by their athletic abilities, most couldn't have hit their wrists. More than likely, they'd have looked up and shanked the slash, maybe nicking an elbow or knuckle, but not with enough force to do serious harm.

Every golf pro daydreams of giving lessons to a beautiful young woman. Don't they? One day, my number came up. I answered a phone call from a young lady whose voice was absolutely enthralling. I mean the phone melted right in my hand.

"Do you give golf lessons?" What a question! What a phone manner!

In my deepest and most professional voice, I responded, "I certainly do."

We set the first lesson for Saturday at 8:00 AM. That morning, the usual inhabitants of the pro shop were assembled and atwitter, waiting to catch a look at my sexy-voiced student. Although it may strike some people as callow and unprofessional, I felt it was my obligation to share the impending appearance of the voice's owner with as many of my golfer pals as possible. I rationalized by saying it would acclimate her to the place and give her a good idea of the camaraderie inspired by the game. Yeah, the Dirty Dozen welcomes you to Swallow's Nest.

Just before 8:00, around the corner came a drop-dead-gorgeous blonde. There was a rush to the windows and a collective sigh. She was beautiful, she was statuesque, she was sexy, and she was heading straight for the pro shop. Be still, my heart. She opened the door. Her voice spoke only to me: "Are you Roly?"

I fought the impulse to sing my answer like they do in Hollywood musicals. Instead, I mumbled, "I certainly am." That was just to show her I can be a slick-talking rascal when the occasion calls for it.

She introduced herself. Her name was Karen. She hardly seemed to mind stepping through the puddles of drool that dripped from the open mouths of my friends in her path. She was a pure beginner in golf, knew nothing about the game, but wanted to learn. Did I think I was the right man to teach her? I certainly did.

I led Karen out to the practice area, partially to escape the stares and heavy breathing in the crowded pro shop. We began with basic theory. The first lesson involved no hitting. We worked on the proper grip, and I gave her a rental club to take home. I watched as she walked away and told myself to "get a grip."

With much anticipation on my part, the day came for Lesson Number Two, and Karen came to the pro shop looking more stunning than the week before. I noticed, but I was a consummate professional, and it was time to get down to business. I poured out a bucket of range balls, opened a bag of new white tees, and announced that today we would hit the ball. I teed one up. Karen swung sweetly but hit nothing. Her grip was great. Try it again, but look at the ball. Another pretty swing; again no contact. She actually swung fairly powerfully for a beginner. There was some promise here. Time for the trained professional to share his vast expertise.

"Okay, Karen," I said, "we're going to put a ball on the turf like this. No tee. You need to whack it and take a divot." I explained what a divot was.

Karen took it all in, then took that trusty 7-iron back and swung it. She fired it into the turf, just the turf behind the ball, not the ball. The blow was about 4.3 on the Richter Scale. We both vibrated from the concussion. Then, in that sexy voice, came perhaps the saddest words I've ever heard as a golf professional: "Divots hurt!"

They certainly do. She left me there on the practice area, never to return. Nothing I could say would offset the hurt she felt. The lonely 7-iron occupied a special place in the pro shop. The rest is a faded memory. It was back to lesser lessons and less glamorous students. I smiled and gave them my best, but Karen had taken a divot out of my heart. She certainly did.

To spark interest and promote play at Swallow's Nest, we formed a Men's Club with handicap events for the members. I started a Beat the Pro competition, a one-day tournament. Anyone who beat me got free beer. The big touring pro takes on everybody in the joint. Piece of cake. Bring on those high handicappers. Unfortunately, the big touring pro was unable to gear down his game that day and knocked it in six water hazards during the round. The entire Men's Club was delirious with delight. Almost everybody beat the Head Swallow, even those who were taking lessons from me. They sent out for an extra keg.

All but two of the forty members trounced me. The two losers threatened to quit the club. I begged them to stay; I needed someone I could beat.

Swallow's Nest was home to me for four years. The course grew and improved. The membership was great to me. Every time I'd play in a tournament somewhere, there'd be a Swallow's Nest member in the gallery, telling everyone he could beat me. My reign as Head Swallow was indeed a high honor and a special privilege.

A complete set of mentors.

I have been blessed with many mentors. First and foremost was my father. Then at Thorny Lea there was Max Wind, who helped me with college, and the Toscas.

John Tosca, known as "Junior", had a profound influence on me when I was a teen. He was a ruggedly handsome six-footer with a crewcut and a permanent tan, and he was very much his own man. A Holy Cross graduate, Junior had been captain of the golf team. When I was at Thorny Lea, he was the Massachusetts State Amateur Champion. It was instructive and inspirational for me to watch him play and to play with him. Our scores were not far apart, but I was never the player that he was.

When I was granted a membership at Thorny Lea, it was kind of a scholarship to help me develop as a golfer. I was only a kid, and the prospect of stepping up socially and golf-wise made me initially apprehensive. Up stepped John Tosca, Jr., current state amateur champ, to greet me and take me under his wing. He introduced me around, showed me the ropes, and genuinely befriended me.

John always treated me as an equal…which I definitely was not. He always made sure I was included with a seat at the table in the men's lounge; always waved me over to join the group that sat around the cheddar cheese and saltines. These were the studs, the best players who made the club outstanding, and gentleman John was the best stud of all. He was my confidant about golf and sometimes about growing into manhood, and he truly cared.

He's the one who got me into the games with the big boys. Like a protective father, he made sure I didn't get into the wrong games. I knew by the look on his face what to avoid and when I was doing the right thing. Most importantly, Junior never judged me.

Our relationship continued throughout my college years. It reached an ultimate point when we went head to head in the Brockton City Open Championship. After 54 holes, we were dead-even. The following week, there was an 18-hole playoff at Thorny Lea with a gallery of about one thousand people. As I recall, it was a terrific match, and the better player prevailed. Junior won. Afterward, with incredible style and thoughtfulness, he told reporters that he had been lucky to beat me, that with a few breaks I could have won. I don't think so. I couldn't have beaten him, and it was an honor to have been beaten by him.

Tom LoPresti was another of my memorable mentors. Concerning Swallow's Nest, he used to ask, "How do you like that little roller-skating rink?" LoPresti was the godfather of golf pros in northern California, a real mover and shaker. He knew everybody and could do you some good or do you in. It was a mistake to get on his wrong side. For whatever reason, he liked me.

Tom was from the old school, but he literally created a new school. He came from the caddy ranks, learned his trade in the backrooms of pro shops, and ended up as the head professional at Sacramento's largest municipal golf course, Haggin Oaks.

Although slight in stature, he was a man and a businessman not to be taken lightly. Thus the nickname "The Godfather."

He was among the first golf pros in the country to understand the concepts of product merchandising and capturing a market. He bought out inventories from the finest manufacturers and offered top-notch clubs and golf products to California pros at exceptional prices. God forbid that any pro would double-deal or misuse Tom's generosity. I know of one golf professional who tried it and, as a consequence, decided to leave the business.

Tom was a true Italian. When he talked, he used his hands. He embellished his stories with hand gestures. When Tom held court which happened continually, no one else uttered a word. Everyone merely nodded their concurrence. His old-school background made him think big, but watch small details.

It was not unusual for this self-made millionaire to bounce used golf balls on the pavement to see if they had any life left before offering a nickel apiece for the balls. However, he had another side...a side he didn't publicize. Without anyone knowing, he quietly supported down-and-out friends financially. If you were down on your luck and were his pal, Tom LoPresti took care of you.

He was fiercely loyal to those who were loyal to him. It is my conservative estimate that 90% of all the golf pros within 100 miles of Sacramento were beholden to Tommy, either as graduates of his employment or as recipients of his generosity. Still, he bounced the balls on the pavement despite his wealth. Bobby Lunn, former U.S. Publinx Champion in the 1950s, owed his career on the PGA Tour to Tommy, who partially sponsored him. And Tommy's influence got him the rest of what Lunn needed.

To say the least, the man had his idiosyncrasies. In amateur tournaments around Sacramento, Tom usually put out a jar of free tees. The jar opening was just big enough to put your hand in, but perfectly sized to prevent getting your hand out if you tried to grab a handful. You took his free tees a few at a time with your fingertips. Conversely, if a tournament needed several thousand dollars in order to happen, the money mysteriously appeared from an anonymous donor. We all knew the donor was Tommy. He never admitted it, but he never denied it either.

That's how he was...one of a kind.

A young, funny Italian named Ray Lenzi came to work for LoPresti. Now there were two headstrong Italians under the same roof. While all his other employees gave the Godfather a wide berth, Ray loved to needle Tommy at every opportunity. Like the flea on the elephant, Lenzi amused Tom. LoPresti liked Lenzi and loved the stone-breaking. I think Ray was the son Tommy never had, and their affectionate locker-room insults to each other were the lifeblood of their relationship.

Ray Lenzi graduated from shop clerk to become the golf professional at Haggin Oaks. He had an insatiable desire for inside knowledge about the golf swing and studied the mechanics of the swing seriously. He was one of Tommy's teachers and became one of the most knowledgeable teachers I've ever known. Mention the name Ray Lenzi to a Sacramento golfer and you'll get a quizzical look. Mention the name to any of Lenzi's students and they'll all tell you he belongs in the PGA Hall of Fame.

I became the alternate target for his ever-present needle. My lessons with Ray always started with: "You dumb goddamn Frenchman, you still haven't got it right!" After the obligatory insults, he'd move on to the gist of the lesson, then we'd sit for hours and laugh and talk golf. When I was head pro at Swallow's Nest and he was the head pro at Napa Valley C.C., we'd sit for hours in one another's pro shop on days off and discuss the golf swing. The friendly insults that flew both ways were only the entry fee into our exceptional friendship.

Tom LoPresti was my mentor in the sense that he took care of me and saw to it that I was supplied. He always made sure I had as many golf shirts and sets of clubs as I needed. Once, in a moment of seriousness, he said to me, "Frog, you ought to get out of this business. You've got too much class for it." I have no clue why and where that came from.

Lenzi is one of the best fundamental teaching pros I have ever known. On many occasions, he has analyzed and corrected glitch in my game. However, he has never been a great player. LoPresti would watch Ray's practice swings and comment, "Lenzi, if daisies were golf balls, you'd be the U.S. Open champion."

Throughout my career, Ray was always available and helpful, always just a phone call away. After a bad round when I was at the PGA Qualifying School in Florida, I called Ray in California. Although he was 2,000 miles away, Ray understood the problem and straightened me out. It usually took him less than two minutes. Of course, the phone analysis always began: "You dumb goddamn Frenchman, you still haven't got it right!" I wish everyone a mentor like Ray. If you're as lucky as I've been, your mentor will also turn out to be your best friend. Here's to Ray Lenzi, a wonderful gentleman. Daisies or golf balls, he's the best.

It may seem strange to you that I would include my wife here in a description of my mentors, but it makes sense to me because, for the past 30-odd years, she's probably been my greatest mentor. Her understanding, love, and support have made it possible for me to pursue my golf interests at every stage of my adult life.

It happened in the military in the 60s. While teaching navigation at Mather Air Force Base in California, I met a little blonde. She was equally a product of Alabama and Sacramento, and she was dating one of my students, a former Air Force Academy football player. Turned out he had a girl at home, and while he was figuring out whether to zig or zag, I slid in there with my frog-like charm. It was love at first sight...for me.

Beverly, a quiet, beautiful young woman, gave me a break and tentatively agreed to date me at least once. On the first date, I told he that I wanted to marry her. That's what comes of dating inexperience; I was a little premature. Her response was: "You Air Force guys are all alike!"

She left to work in Southern California. I went to visit her every weekend. The economics of weekly travel were murdering my budget, so I convinced Beverly to come back to Sacramento and marry me...several months after we first met. This incredible whirlwind romance started at the end of 1965 and ended with our wedding in April of 1966.

We said our vows in front of a priest with all my Air Force buddies attending in their dress-white uniforms. There were ten fly-boys with sabers, called to attention by "the Teenage Major", a friend named Al Britton. This honor guard formed the arch of swords when the command "Present arms!" was given. With some trepidation, Bev and I walked under the arch. I knew these guys and sensed the danger we were exposed to...particularly after a previous night of hard-drinking hilarity. As we got to the end, I whispered to my new bride, "Watch this. Britton has no clue what the command is to lower the sabers." Then we heard my Major friend give the command: "Cool it!" The swords were returned to their scabbards.

Bev has put up with my shenanigans for 37 years. She's stuck by me through happy highs and spirit-stifling lows. I think about our vows occasionally...and I always think the same thing: "Boy! Did I get the best of that deal." I call her S.O.B....affectionately...it stands for Sweet Old Bev. Believe me, she knows how to cool it.

You're probably wondering if old Bev plays golf. She does, and she could have been pretty good if she had the time to play more than occasionally. Don't forget, she had a full-time job on her hands, raising me for 37 years.

A few years back, she made her annual appearance in the local Board of Realtors golf tournament. It was a scramble format with some sort of applied handicap system that artificially equalizes all the teams. Not exactly the U.S. Open.

Because I am such a popular guy, I wasn't invited to play or even attend the barbeque afterward. So I did what any good husband who wants his wife to have a good time would do; I stayed home, ordered a pizza, and watched a ballgame on the tube.

Around 9:00 PM, I heard the front door open, and into the family room came Beverly, holding a huge trophy. Avoiding eye contact with me, she marched to the fireplace and cleared the mantle. Pushing my most prized mementoes aside, she ceremoniously placed her huge, ostentatious trophy in the center of the mantle, the place of honor for such awards in our home. She turned slowly, glared at me glaring at her, and said, "When's the last time you won a tournament, big boy?"

What goes around comes around. That's the kind of thing that's made our marriage work.

These then are my mentors. There are others later in my life, just as important in their influence on me. It is truly amazing, the number of people who have had an extraordinary positive effect on my life. I regard them all as the best in my life.

Big shot.

As in real life, there are contradictions in golf. It's a kid's game. It can be played and enjoyed into old age, probably more than any other game or sport. Competitive golf is a young man's game. It's a game for all ages. I added a whole new category for tour pro want-to-bes...life-long obsession.

From my final round on the tour after my sponsor was taken away, I kept on hoping for a reprieve, a miracle, anything that would return me to competitive golf at the highest level. Playing on the tour was the ultimate anticipation of my life, and I had waited for it through four years of college and six years of military service. That long wait had developed a callused expectation within me. It didn't allow for comprehension of failure. To get a taste of the tour and be on and off it in such a short time seemed a supremely cruel joke. The cavalry was surely on its way; help had to be just over the next hill. Even when help didn't show up, when I had to get a job, even then I clung to my desired destiny. I kept casting about for ways to salvage the situation because I wasn't ready to accept reality. I was in denial. I hoped and waited a long time, too long, and it shaded my life.

Bev, my staunchest supporter, realized the fantasy was over.

She knew we'd have to move on with our life. I didn't. I thought that whatever we needed had to come from golf. Of course I regarded each successive job as only temporary while I thrashed around and waited for the cavalry to rescue me. Everything I tried turned out to frustrate me. Every avenue of opportunity turned into a dead end. It was Catch 22 and deja vu. The PGA informed me that I'd have to go back to Players School because of my lack of winnings...even though I wasn't on the tour to win any winnings. Potential backers popped up, but dematerialized when it came time to put up.

For a long time it was painful for me to even watch a tour event on TV, let alone attend as part of the gallery. When I did watch a major on television, I saw my college counterparts... Frank Beard, Homero Blancas, Tommy Aaron...guys I knew I could play with. Why wasn't I out there? Why did I have to be a working stiff?

It reached a point where, if I had been a prizefighter, they'd have stopped the fight because I was so badly beaten. And I would have begged to continue because I was the only one who didn't realize it. In my battered brain, I'd have been sure I was only taking a standing eight count. I'd have been certain I'd get 'em in a later round. In a sense, I was punchy; that's what you get when you combine competitive stubbornness with denial.

Life went on, but where was I going? Driving range to assistant pro to Head Swallow to what to where? As it was happening, I didn't realize that my four years at Swallow's Nest would be my last career move in golf. Being a club professional was not my dream. The long-term pay-off and satisfaction didn't happen for me. At that point, when I checked the score card for my life, it didn't add up.

We all grow out of certain phases and preoccupations in our lives. My occupation and preoccupation with golf was affecting my personal progress and my family's right to a better deal. Eventually, it dawned on me that I'd have to find another way to make a better living. It was difficult to give up the golf dream that started when I was a boy, but I set out on another course...reluctantly.

In the early 1970s, I got into the beer business. And it got into me. It was my first job out of golf, and it certainly didn't help my fondness for drinking. I moved on from the business, but not from the beer.

For the next fifteen years, I made my way on the middle-management road as a sales executive with various nationwide trucking companies. "Hey, Roly from Ryder is here. He was on the PGA Tour once. Let's go to lunch with him and have a few laughs. He has some great stories." I got into the habit of having a few drinks with my clients. It provided temporary relief from my own unhappiness with myself and my line of business. I sat there thinking: *I shouldn't be doing this. I belong on the Tour, not in the trucking business.* Roly, the Realist. Let's have one more round.

Once in a while, I'd catch a rerun of a local television show that had been aired the last day of the U.S. Open in 1969. The Sacramento station had done a half-hour documentary about my brief career on the pro tour. It was entitled: *So you want to be a golf pro?* One segment always made my eyes moist. It was an interview with Bev and Michelle, seated on the couch in our home. When asked her feelings about the end of my opportunity on the Tour, Bev replied, "When I watched Roly coming down the final hole at Spyglass Hill, I knew our dream was gone. I had tears in my eyes." It made my heart cry.

Through it all, Beverly has been the best part of my life and the greatest wife a husband has ever been graced with. She has given me unconditional love and my daughter Michelle, who has always been my pride and joy. For much of my life, I missed the point that God had given me everything a normal person could want. But I wasn't normal. I was selfish. I needed more; I wanted the Tour.

My self-inflicted martyrdom outlasted all my job changes and business ventures. To survive middle age, I was forced into some sound decisions and sane actions. In 1986, I realized that I had more than a minor problem with drink. I admitted to myself that I was an alcoholic, went to AA, and worked at gaining control over that insidious addiction. It worked, and I've been sober and determined ever since. As always, the experience gave me some good with the bad. It imposed humility on me, and taught me compassion for others. I desperately needed a healthy dose of both.

It's too bad that there's not some similar program for other obsessions. There was never a day that went by when I didn't think of playing professional golf. I fantasized about my abilities and dreamed of the golfing riches I was certain I could win. If I could figure out how to do it, I'd head straight for the PGA Tour. Oops, past fifty and too old? Then I'd head for the Senior Tour...or the Senior Senior Tour...whatever. That was my mindset as I wobbled through life. As with alcohol, I didn't realize how it affected me. I thought I was being shortstopped by circumstance from becoming a big shot on the Tour.

A playing partner sent by Providence.

It took a genuine big shot to end Roly's folly. I met an extraordinary man who changed my outlook and helped me change my life with a single, incisive, profound comment. Ironically, it happened on a golf course, convincing evidence that God shares my locker-room sense of humor. The man was a new friend, Brian Buffini. At the time, we didn't know each other well, but he has since become the teaching pro I trust for the game of life. Here's how it happened:

As with most of the good things that I have found, my wife led me to Brian. Bev is a realtor, and she went to the Providence seminars that Brian conducts for business professionals. During intense two-day sessions called *Turning Point Retreats*, he teaches his system of selling exclusively by referral. In reality, he teaches much more...how to improve your life as well as your business...how to manage yourself and your abilities...how to be the best that you can be in all respects. But I didn't know all that at first.

Bev came back bubbling and bursting with enthusiasm for the program. She said it was just what I needed; it would do me a world of good; Brian Buffini had a better way to approach life.

I said, "Bull!", but Bev badgered me into going to one of Brian's sessions. As usual when it involved something that might do me some good, I went reluctantly...very reluctantly. I was the prototypical jaded husband being dragged to a self-betterment session by my beknighted wife. Humbug! Self-improvement seminars, all the same, smoke and snake oil...I knew what to expect. I hadn't just fallen off some flaming fairway tractor.

Imagine my surprise when I found myself interested, then intrigued, and finally into it all the way. It took a while because I fancy myself a hard sell. What else would you expect from a New England Yankee who sells for a living? I sat there with my guard up and my arms folded across my chest. I listened hard for phony baloney. I was determined not to be taken in by the clever devices they use to manipulate an audience. Whatever else I was, Roly the Reluctant was not an easy mark. There would be no samba-line seminar shenanigans with me.

Right off the bat, I noticed a few things that warranted suspicion. Brian Buffini was young, somewhere in his middle thirties. What was I going to learn from a kid nearly half my age? And he was from Ireland. And he had a brogue. What did he know about Americans and selling in America? He was engaging and he made sense, but they're all charmers and they all have a line, don't they now. Brian Buffini was sharp...and a lot slicker than I was. He did have a great delivery and a terrific sense of humor that set well with me, but I kept waiting for him to try to sell me the Brooklyn Bridge. He didn't, and I started to pay more beneficial attention.

He talked about moving through change in our lives in stages...from survival to stability to success and ultimately to significance. His definition of significance was using our individual abilities, our gifts, to help ourselves so that we could then help others. Everything he said made a lot of sense to me. I could see that everyone in the audience was into it.

By the end of the first day, I was all the way into what the young Irishman was selling. Brian Buffini was inspiring hope and commitment and determination to change for the better. And oh, by the way...he was telling you how to do it while he showed you how to improve your business. And he was making you laugh...at yourself reflected in the pratfalls of others...and at his own mistakes and missteps.

I learned a lot about him. Brian grew up economically disadvantaged in Dublin. He was the son of a seventh-generation house painter and had four brothers and a sister. He'd immigrated from Ireland to San Diego with no money and survived a serious accident that almost crippled him. When he recovered, he painted houses, worked in a FotoMat, and scrambled through a succession of jobs to make a living. He became a realtor and a millionaire, utilizing the referral system he developed and now teaches to business people all across the country. Brian married an Olympian. Beverly Robinson Buffini was a member of the 1988 U.S. Volleyball Team, and she is a dynamic speaker and motivator in her own right. They have six children and a wonderful family life.

Beverly inspired Brian to fully realize his speaking abilities, and together they founded Providence Systems to teach and coach others to realize and use their abilities to the fullest...to improve their businesses and lives...to help others. There were no big secrets to it; just get out of your own way and fully utilize your natural gifts. From a company of five persons in the early 1990s, Providence has grown into the largest and most successful business coaching company in America with over 200 employees. Everybody can use some one-on-one coaching to help them achieve their goals. As a former teaching pro, I knew that was true. The Buffinis and their company were phenomenal.

It was great that Brian was entertaining and made me laugh. It was better that he was a normal guy, a good egg, human and approachable. It was even better that he was genuine. It was enlightening. I came away from the seminar with a wealth of information and a new outlook. Old Bev was right again. Without knowing that we'd become friends in the future, I became an advocate of Brian Buffini. But what I really still wanted most was to be on the Tour. And I continued to bemoan the fact that I wasn't playing competitive professional golf for a living. And it was getting later and later in my life. Roly the Unrealistic was one stubborn sunuvagun.

Fate arranged it so that Brian Buffini and I played a round of golf together, just the two of us. Brian has a single-digit handicap and could be close to a scratch player if he had the time to devote to golf. While we played, we talked about the Tour and I told him my experiences. I did most of the talking. He listened with great interest to my stories about the Players' School, the Monday-morning qualifying routine, and the events. I told him about my backer's big check, the man's death the next day, the check returned, the dream lost. My long-suffering martyrdom surely showed in everything I said.

Finally, feeling super-sorry for myself, I said, "When I die, I'm going to ask God why He did that to me."

Looking me right in the eye as if he'd been waiting years for the opportunity to set me straight, Brian responded, "Better you should ask God why He gave you so many gifts."

It was like a paralyzing punch in the gut, and it was the best thing that could have happened to me. Brian had given me the answer I needed. He was right. It was the key that opened the door to the rest of my life. I immediately felt that my fight with myself for the past 35 years was finally over. Knockout! No count necessary. Roly, the self-destroying martyr from Massachusetts, was ready to hang up his self-pity.

I instantly knew I had the answer I'd searched for a long time. Brian saw my relief and acceptance in my eyes and body language. In empathy and friendship, he reinforced his words by putting his hand on my shoulder. What an unexpected moment and a strange setting for such a momentous event in my life! On a golf course after a great round at the end of a very pleasant day. I started talking about myself and ended up feeling complete for the first time in a long, long time. Brian Buffini, a bright young man many years my junior, sets me straight by saying something I should have known myself. As I have already said, God has a great sense of humor.

That humor extends far beyond me as a target and strikes the most gifted and successful of people. It should be obvious that I have a deep respect and affection for young, gifted, successful Mr. Buffini. However, in a display of heavenly equal-opportunity humor, God has goosed Brian on numerous occasions, and I love Brian's self-deprecating stories about it...one in particular because it has to do with golf.

Because Brian is a teacher and a caring father, and dedicated to making yourself the best person you can be, he decided it was time for his two older children to learn the fundamentals of his own recreational passion...golf. Start them young; teach them early; lead by example...all that good stuff. Brian's advice is: "Don't bother telling them what to do. They're too busy watching what you do." His kids are all champs with incredible motivation. He and his wife have encouraged them to pursue all challenges. So they learned proper grip and correct swing mechanics. During their instruction, their dad stressed the points of etiquette and behavior vital to the game. No talking while someone else is over a shot. Don't step in anyone's line. No running ahead. And most importantly, no displays of frustration and anger. The kids were ready. They played with their dad and behaved beautifully. There was not one breach of golf etiquette in nine holes.

Shortly thereafter, Brian and his brothers were playing an eighteen-hole family match. The Buffini brothers are very competitive and take their golf seriously. And they each have their on-course idiosyncrasies.

Gary, the oldest and a fine player, sometimes finishes his swing in the "altar boy genuflection" position, possibly because of his early religious upbringing. Kevin, the youngest, called "Tin Cup", has never seen a lake or tree he couldn't clear with his shot. Dermot is also a fine golfer and the on-course comedian. And they all know how to stir the pot and stick a barb into their brothers.

Brian, it turns out, is not perfect. From my own experience, I know that it's hard to hold in all your gifts on a golf course. For one thing, he never feathers a fairway shot; his swing is always set to nuke it. And now and then, he demonstrates the peculiar system he's developed to relieve tension after a bad shot. While it happens only occasionally, Brian has been known to lose his temper and toss a club. To be totally honest, he's a leader in this, as he is in everything he does. I'm sure he holds the record for the longest, highest club throw ever recorded on earth. His record will only be broken on a planet with significantly less gravitational pull.

Back to the match, near the end. The Buffini boys were coming down the final hole. I'm virtually positive they were playing for knee. Gary, Dermot and Kevin had hit to the green, and it was Brian's shot. Fairway nuke coming! Brian nailed one at the

18th green. Like a jet fighter taking off, his ball roared past the flag and started to climb. When last seen, it was clearing the kiddies' wading pool by the clubhouse.

As chance would have it, Beverly had brought the Buffini children to the club. Just before Brian's shot, they had positioned themselves behind the 18th green to watch their uncles and father in action.

"There's Daddy!" cried Anna...just as Brian let his club fly. They all watched its incredible aerodynamic journey across the bright blue sky. So much for etiquette and exemplary behavior and fatherly failings.

Later that evening, as the Buffinis gathered at the dinner table, Anna was selected to say grace: "God bless our family, and the food we are about to eat...and, God, please help my Daddy so he won't get mad and throw his golf club anymore."

Her Daddy added an embarrassed "Amen."

The frog finds his lily pad.

When you don't get enough of something you want, you always want more. That's a normal human reaction, and that's exactly what my problem was. I felt I had missed a lot. There was a huge absence in me from my cut-short time on the PGA Tour. And there's probably an equally large empty space between my ears for hanging on to my personal dream too long. You would think that I'd be happy, having played on the pro Tour and all. You'd wonder why I wasn't satisfied with the great life I'd had with golf as the centerpiece. You wouldn't believe my obsession and emotions in the grasp of Tour golf madness. I look back at it now and regard it as debilitating and unrealistic. It had a very strong hold on me, and it clouded my judgment and outlook in many ways.

Working for a living outside the golf business was okay, but it certainly was hard to keep my golfing skills sharp, and it was difficult to schedule my time for tournaments. Keep in mind that, before Brian Buffini changed my outlook, I still believed I should be there, teeing it up with the Tour guys. So what if years had passed? And skills had slipped a bit? So what if Jack Nicklaus had graduated to the Senior Tour?

As I approached sixty, I maintained the abiding belief that I would emerge from golfing purgatory and win some event. This would be accomplished without a plan and with little or no real effort on my part...miraculously. It would vindicate my displaced life and validate my true profession. When and where was this miracle supposed to take place? Hell, I didn't know. It was just gonna happen. In my befogged brain, the details didn't matter. It was just supposed to happen, that's all. And I wasn't getting any younger!

This was my grand delusion. Age didn't alter it, and common sense couldn't put a crack in it...until Brian came along. He had the ability to move me to action and make my goals seem attainable. I had been waiting for a limo to pick me up; I should have caught the bus to reality...or the senior bus, whichever came first.

I made some choices that were good for me, and I had some great support and help to do that. Judy Hummerich, my personal coach at Providence, played a large part in inching me forward. She alternated between gently nudging me and kicking my butt in all the right directions. It took about four years because I had to overcome my built-in resistance to common sense and my reluctance to adhere to a system. It all seemed so ordinary and mundane; could it really apply to me, the Extraordinary Roly? Most of us consider ourselves unique and believe the ordinary doesn't apply to us. I am living proof that it's a false belief. I was my own portable, take-it-with-you-everywhere, self-defeating obstacle. By now, I'm sure you're sure that I wasn't aware that I was my own worst enemy. Slowly but surely, Judy and Brian set me straight. They helped me learn to get out of my own way and to make measured progress. They got me on track to a point where life was good again.

Judy coached my wife and me. It was no small undertaking. Husbands and wives don't always communicate their problems. I didn't know that at one point my Beverly was struggling in her real estate business. Judy talked with her frequently, provided a sympathetic ear, and offered solid suggestions. All the while, I wasn't aware of my wife's dilemma.

One day early in the morning, our phone rang and Bev answered it. She said hello and listened, but gave no indication who was on the other end. The call was brief. Bev said, "Thank you" and hung up with tears in her eyes.

Fearing some bad news, I asked, "What's the matter? Who was that? Is anything wrong?"

Bev replied, "It was Judy. She said she loved me and hang in there."

We talked, and Bev told me about her business struggles. She felt she was back on track again and praised Judy for her astute and caring assistance. We were both relieved and the better for Bev's unburdening.

That afternoon, it was my turn for Judy's bi-weekly coaching call. However, it was not my turn for any "I love you." Sweet and gentle, caring Judy was in my face and all over me because I hadn't done what I promised to do during our previous session.

She chewed me out like a drill sergeant reprimanding a recruit.

I knew she was right. To take the pressure off, I kidded Judy: "How come you tell Bev you love her, but you beat me like a drum?"

Her reply was short and to the point: "I love you, too. Now get off your butt and get going!" She had gotten to know me so well. She instinctively knew that a kick was more effective than a kiss at that moment. Thanks, Judy. I love you, too. You've helped me change my life for the better.

I truly began my metamorphosis in December of 2000 at one of Brian's Turning Point Retreats in Carmel, surrounded by more than 2,500 attending business professionals. It was the time in the session when everyone quietly writes their goals. The process of writing your goals down on paper has an almost mystical effect in bringing them about; I've seen the results validate the process.

I set a goal to lose 30 pounds in the coming year; to rehab my chronically aching back; to increase my business by at least 100%. And I set a goal to win a significant golf tournament. All my goals were ongoing for the year 2001 with specific dates for accomplishment. I had decided it was time to do more than get out of my own way. It was time to take action and get Roly rolling.

I went back into Weight Watchers and began the melting process. With Judy's coaching, I set guidelines for business growth. She made me live up to my promises, and my annual increase was close to 150%.

My back problems were difficult. Every night as I watched television, I did stretching exercises and strengthening drills. I worked to get rid of the gut we all acquire as we hit later middle age. Slowly, I began to see results. I never achieved the washboard look, but I began to look and feel better. One of my friends remarked, "Roly, you're a cockroach turning into a butterfly." That made me feel better about myself.

After staying away from tournament golf and the realities of life for several decades, I had committed to take both up again. The golf was problematic. Have you ever noticed that when you play a sport just for fun, it's not too tough? But when you focus on improving, it becomes much more difficult.

My financial planning business kept me pretty busy, but I found I could work my own hours and arrange my time to play in tournaments. In the second half of the year 2000, I had started to play in some senior tournaments in northern California, where I live. Most of the senior players were top-notch amateurs. A California top player is truly a top player. And these men were gracious and hospitable. They welcomed me warmly into their group of white-haired fat-bellies, all of whom were players. Before my goal-setting in Carmel, I entered a few tournaments and surprisingly won the County Championship with three under par for the two rounds. It felt terrific, but it just whet my appetite.

After Carmel, while rounding into shape, I played a few tournaments early in the year with only moderate success. I worked on my game and finished fifth in the Northern California Golf

Association Senior Championship. That was a biggie for me because it gave me an exemption into the California State Amateur, Senior Division. Buoyed by this success, I won a couple of lesser senior events. My initial goal for golf was accomplished. I was now a noticeable factor on the senior golf scene, and I was truly enjoying myself...the way I should have all along. It had taken 61 years, but this old Frog had finally found his lily pad.

I was looking forward to the California State Amateur at Pebble Beach. The time came, and we came back to the place where my pro career had come apart. How different it was from that sad ending many years ago. This time I was delighted to be in the field, playing with former champions who were my friends, enjoying them and the moment.

Bev and I have always viewed the Monterey Peninsula as a special place. We arrived a couple of days early and did typical tourist things. I bought a tie in a chic Carmel boutique; everybody needs a $60 silk tie with the emblematic Lone Cypress on it. We took a ride along the scenic coast and marveled at its awesome beauty. The weather was perfect, sea lions were barking, whales were breaching, and God was smiling. How could you not enjoy it? My changed attitude made everything seem better and made me aware of my blessings.

The first round was played on Wednesday. I was in a foursome with my pal, Clyde Berg, and two golfers from southern California. I guess I was glad to be there and it showed in my play. Birdying the 18th, I finished with a three-under 69. While I floated around in bliss at leading the tournament, Clyde, an incorrigible practical joker, was busy building me a reputation I didn't deserve.

Walking off the last green, a Monterey golf writer requested an interview, and I told him I'd be back for it. While I was turning in our scorecards, Clyde was engaged in an animated conversation with the writer. When I came back for my interview, Clyde bowed out quickly and beat a hasty retreat to the parking lot. I thought it was unusual for him to leave the scene of my potential humiliation.

The sportswriter seemed suspiciously too respectful, almost in awe of my golfing credentials. He reviewed what he knew about me. I had played in five U.S. Opens and four National Amateur finals. I was once the least known, most feared and respected player on the pro tour. Friend and playing partner to the great and the near-great. And that was just the beginning. It was all baloney. I asked the writer who told him all that stuff about me.

"Your playing partner," he said. "Who is that guy?"

Clyde! He'd done it again...supplied the golf writer with a bloated bunch of malarky about me. Just trying to help me out and make me a better-known golfer. It took me half an hour to undo the damage.

There was a cocktail party that night to give out the second-round pairings. I was embarrassed to be in the spotlight as the tournament leader and left early. My embarrassment carried over to the next day as I shot a 75. That put me at even after 36 holes.

When the final day dawned, I had a butterfly or two fluttering around in my belly. Roly the Rock, formerly unshakeable tour pro, was turning into a nervous Nellie. It had been a long time since I'd been in position to win anything significant. After all those years, the old competitiveness was kicking in. I didn't dare dwell on how much I wanted to win; it came across like my last chance. I wasn't that desperate, was I?

I spent about ten minutes in the locker room, pumping myself up, trying to convince myself that I was the best player in the field, that I was going to win. However, the psych approach didn't work for me. Instead, I left the locker room with the resolve that I wasn't going to lose the tournament; someone would have to beat me.

I promptly proceeded to bogey the first hole. Our foursome was defending champ Mike Riley, my buddy Bob Rowland, good friend Dr. Mike Davis, a prominent cardiologist, and me. My adrenaline was up and pumping. After I hit my initial tee shot, I ran down the fairway.

The official on the first tee yelled, "Don't run, Roly, you'll have a heart attack!"

I hollered back, "It's okay. I'm with my cardiologist!"

Dr. Davis commented, "Not today, Frog. You die and I move up one place in the standings." So much for the Hippocritic oath.

By the end of four holes, I was two strokes down. Roly resolve was faltering. It was time for the mystical effects of goal-setting to kick in. With dogged determination, I managed to hit 13 fairways and 15 greens in regulation, keeping within a stroke or two of Riley. I stayed close, and finally we were tied after the 16th hole. Riley was playing solidly, but getting no breaks with his putting. On 17, I stuck a 6-iron fairly close and made par. Mike Riley three-putted a terrible twisting 60-footer.

Pumped up, I crushed my drive almost 300 yards on the par-five final hole. Riley hit it into the right rough, then whacked it to within an easy 9-iron. My second shot into a steady 12 mph wind was 187 yards to the flag which was tucked behind two towering cypress trees. Over 300 spectators were looking down at us from behind the 18th green. Somehow, I spotted Beverly in the crowd. I planned to cut a 3-iron around the trees. I set up with the 3-iron, then stepped away because it entered my mind that I was a hooker, not a fader. I composed myself and visualized the fade, then stepped back to the ball. The hit was so pure that there wasn't any feel of impact, just the club flowing through my follow-through. It was dead solid perfect. It seemed as though the ball stayed in the air for at least two minutes, and I watched its flight with a feeling of pure ecstasy.

The gallery behind the green applauded enthusiastically. Even with the wind in my face, I could hear them cheering. Even at 200 yards, I spotted the smile on Bev's face. The moment was mine.

On the verge of becoming emotional, I looked at my pal, Dr. Davis. He said, "Pal, you did it." He knew the shot was a winner.

I needed to walk by myself to control my feelings. As I strode to the green, at first I was overjoyed. Then I chastised myself for being premature. I reminded myself: 'It's not over yet, you damn jerk!' The applause continued when I reached green. I didn't want to make eye contact with Bev; that would have done me in. We both knew it wasn't the PGA Tour, but right then it was everything we'd invested our younger lives in. It was validation in a very satisfying way.

I had an eight-foot putt for an eagle and just barely managed two putts for the birdie. It gave me a two-under score of 70 and a two-shot victory. That was good enough for me.

At the scorer's table, I could barely think, let alone count. In charge of card turn-in was Judge Bill Giffen, the upcoming NCGA President, and a long-time friend. All cards were in except mine. With a knowing smile, Bill told me, "Take your time. We've got until tomorrow." Finally, after totaling and checking my card ten times, I handed it to Bill.

He stood and declared, "Judge Giffen deems this event complete. Mr. Lamontagne is the new California State Champion." Then he leaned over the table and kissed me on the forehead.

I felt Bev's arm around my shoulder. I turned to her and finally made eye contact. We had done it. It was as much her victory as mine, and it had been a long time coming. Damn, it felt good to be a winner again. Pretty good stuff for an old fart. I had jumped to a helluva lily pad.

Ballzheimer's becomes me.

There is an insidious affliction that all golfers will face someday. It is debilitating. It affects self-esteem. I have named it Ballzheimer's. Some of you have already noticed the early warning signs. The rest of you should be prepared for it because your time is inevitably approaching.

They say there are four progressive indications of losing it to old age for a man. First you forget names. Then you forget faces. Then you forget to zip up. Then you forget to zip down.

What to be alert for? How will you know it is upon you? Usually, the first indication is when you overhear younger players say: "Man, in his day, that old guy could really play." Your first reaction will be to look around to see whom in the hell they're talking about. Your second reaction will be shocked surprise when you realize they're talking about you. Your final reaction will be resentful sadness that you're regarded by the younger set as over the hill. I know because it's happened to me.

Tom Dixon, a good friend and former San Francisco City champion, was labeled a victim of Ballzheimer's some years ago. The comments of younger players actually had a reverse effect. They ticked him off so much that they spurred him to win a few more amateur victories before the disease took over.

Ballzheimer's has many symptoms and side effects that don't involve golf. One is generational lack of understanding. That goes both ways. For example, I can't understand why a young guy with a perfectly good head of hair would shave it all off and go around bald. What's with that? I spend a good part of each morning retrieving every hair that falls out of my head onto the counter or sink. Just as I repair ball marks on the green, I repair every little follicle loss, hoping it will grow back. I want to say to those demeaning youngsters, "Someday you'll be repairing your own hair losses, Junior."

For many years I sported a crew-cut. When people I've known a long time ask why I no longer have that snappy crew-cut, I tell them I had a crew-cut until the crew bailed out. Because it is a sign of aging, I identify hair loss as another sign of Ballzheimer's.

Then there's the vision thing. That's a symptom, too. Or it could be a major contributing factor in the onset of the disease.

Recently I went to the eye doctor. I go to Dr. Benkle because he's an avid golfer and I trust him. I told him I was sure my eyes were weakening. Beyond my need for stronger reading glasses, I was certain I needed new glasses for driving and golfing. I told him I played golf without glasses and admitted that I couldn't determine whether my ball was sitting up or in a thin lie. If anything could be worse than that, when I drove early in the morning, automobile tail lights were nothing more than a red glow to my eyes, creating a dangerous situation.

Dr. Benkle was horrified. Twice he said to me, "I can't believe you're playing golf without wearing your glasses!"

"Yes, and when I drive I can hardly see the cars in front of me," I responded.

To which he responded, "How can you hit an iron properly if you can't distinguish the lie of the golf ball?" He shook his head with angry disbelief. Dr. Benkle was one doctor who had his priorities straight. On the bright side, the older you get, the easier it is to hit the ball out of sight.

Difficulty remembering your priorities is another symptom of Ballzheimer's disease. This can be a two-fold problem: first, you have to remember how to hit the golf ball; second, you have to remember where the ball went. I'm not kidding, loss of short-term memory can play havoc with your game. Sometimes, after a lay-off, I go to the practice range and can't remember what I was working on last time.

This is not completely a downhill trip. There are some benefits from memory loss. One of the best byproducts is an inflated false memory of how good your skills used to be. As you lose it, your memory of your own abilities is embellished. And it seems so real to you.

Ever hear one of your old friends reminisce about how far he used to hit his driver? By damn, for every year that's gone by, he's gotten ten yards longer than he actually was. By the time he's 70 years of age, he'll actually believe that he used to hit his tee shots 300+ yards. And that will have been before metal drivers. Wow! If he lives to be 80, he will have been the greatest player of his time, unrecognized of course. Not only will he have been the secret long-driving champ, but he'll remember himself as a wonderful ball-striker. In fact, if he had also been a great putter, he'll probably be convinced that he could have been one of the truly great players. All this from a guy who hit it 215 yards off the tee with the wind behind him on his best day. Ballzheimer's is a strange, mind-altering affliction.

The side effects can be good and bad. If you threw clubs to vent your anger when you were younger, now it's not the thing to do, but not for reasons of good behavior or decorum on course. Now, throwing a club usually results in injury to yourself: inflammation of the rotator cuff, muscle pulls, stiff neck, problems with shoulders or lower back. Throw a club, and you risk one or all of the above. While the act is a release of anger, it also requires energy. As a result of your progressive debilitation, you may not have that much energy to throw away.

Sadly, another side effect is total lack of accuracy with the club throw. As we get older, directional control becomes a severe problem. And it becomes harder to remember to fling the club in the direction of your last shot. There is a tendency to throw it toward the hole, not toward the mishit ball. There are also problems with timing and tempo. Again due to debilitation, geezer golfers tend to let go too fast or hold on too long. Like a little helicopter, the spinning shaft can go out of control. I've seen it boomerang back on the thrower. It could injure a playing partner or bystander. Then there is the horrible humiliation of having to retrieve the club.

As I said, finding out you have Ballzheimer's can throw you for a loop. Comments from others can make it worse. There is a "piling on" principle that applies from those nearest and dearest to you. After lengthy consideration and with great hesitation because it might frighten her concerning my mental health, I confided my Ballzheimer's symptoms to my wife. Beverly's response was caringly cruel. She smiled knowingly and said, "Senility should be a short and painless trip for you."

As much as I give it out, I get it back two for one. Sometimes I feel like a straight man for The Master Comedian upstairs. For my most recent body renovation, I tried to get in shape by making early morning visits to my local gym. Do you realize there are many deranged individuals at gyms at 5:00 in the morning? I include myself among them.

There I was, baggy sweats, baggy body and nice golf cap, chugging along briskly on the treadmill. Speed set at 4 mph, very challenging for me, working up to a full sweat. Suddenly, an announcement over the loudspeaker: car with license plate SIX ONES has its headlights on. My car. My vanity plates reflecting six holes-in-one, eat your heart out. Damn! Without shutting off the treadmill, I jumped off the machine, went outside, and turned my lights off.

I made my way back in through a bevy of cute yuppy wives in

ponytails. They had arrived for their early-morning workout while their husbands made breakfast. With no thought of impressing them, I jumped with both feet onto the speeding treadmill.

Oops! Both feet shot backwards. Mayday! Mayday! I was going down...but not without a fight. My right hand grabbed the machine's railing. Had to try to stabilize myself. Oh, oh, wrong move. Now my body was twisting and torqueing. I was on my way down butt-first. Unable to release my death-grip, I was being depantsed by the treadmill. Oh, the embarrassment! I had to let go because the machine was winning the contest of skin against moving plastic ramp. When I let go, the machine got angry and fired me off its back.

It's difficult to maintain your dignity while you're being shot out of a treadmill with your sweatpants around your ankles. Not one bobbing ponytail looked my way, but I'll bet I was the butt of some funny stories at the kids' soccer game that day.

Blessed are they who laugh at themselves...for they shall never cease to be amused.

As I approached my golfing twilight years, I continued to play with younger players and particularly enjoyed being able to stay up with them. Golf can be cruel, but it can also be kind to the elderly. Occasionally, it provides a twist of ironic justice. One such sweet moment took place in 1989 at the qualifying for the California State Amateur. I was pitted against all the hotshot professional amateurs, college stars, and kids roughly half my age.

Appropriately, I was in the last qualifying foursome at

Discovery Bay Country Club. That made us the final group to finish the 36 holes. I was one over par which put me well within the score needed to play at Pebble Beach. Coming off the last green, an official asked me what I shot. When I told him, he informed me, "You're in. Please turn your card in right away because they have ten players waiting to play off for the final positions and the alternate slots."

After I checked my card, signed it and turned it in, I walked by the first tee on my way to the parking lot. There was a gaggle of young players waiting for the start of their playoff. They were discussing the top qualifiers. As I passed them, one college-aged kid asked loudly, "Did that old guy, Lamontagne, make it?"

Someone answered, "Yes."

Next came the sweetest words I'd heard since I almost blew out all the candles on my 50th birthday cake. Another of the young wonders chimed in, "Damn. When is that old fart gonna put his clubs away and stay home and mow the lawn?"

Thank you for the unintended compliment. It was just what I needed just when I needed it most. I was the oldest guy to qualify, and I lasted two rounds. When I was ousted after the round of sixteen, I was not unhappy with my performance. In fact, as I was leaving, when I walked by the deserted first tee, I yelled back over my shoulder, "Not bad for an old fart, hey boys!"

Over the years, I have collected disrespect from a wide range of golfing buddies, young and old alike. They demonstrate their lack of respect for me, and I thrive on it. One of the best examples of this synergy came during a local senior event from that senior friend of mine, Clyde Berg. He was once a pro football player with the Dallas Cowboys and has the bad knees, bad back, and assorted aches and pains to prove it. Clyde also is a near-professional practical joker with a locker-room sense of humor.

The two-day event was one of my first tournaments as a certified senior amateur, and I was determined to play well. I needed reconfirmation of my abilities the way some old studs need Rogaine or Viagra. After the first day, I was in the lead. Clyde was a shot or two back, so on the final day, he was playing in the group immediately in front of mine.

At the end of the front nine, I was still in the lead but I was starting to leak oil. And I was adding to my own anxieties. Worried about the wheels coming off my game, I was demonstrating all the signs of patriotic paranoia: my knuckles were turning white, my nails were turning blue, and my eyes were getting red. These were the indications of competitive aging. The white knuckles demonstrated extreme tension; red eyes indicated high blood pressure; and the blue fingernails showed that I was not taking in enough oxygen. In fact, I was scarcely breathing because I was so tightly wrapped. I had forgotten how much fun competitive golf could be.

On the tenth tee, a tough par five where play slowed, we waited for the foursome in front to hit their second shots. Clyde, the longest driver in his group, hit last and hopped in his cart.

Instead of driving toward the green, he turned the cart around and came back toward us, heading down the middle of the fairway directly to the tee. I was ready to hit, but couldn't because Clyde was coming straight at me. It wouldn't do to bean a friend with a drive in your first Senior event.

I stood there, driver in hand, wondering what was compelling Clyde to do this. We were all wondering. No one spoke as he drove straight up to me. He stopped just in front of the tee, squinted at me, and said, "I've been watching you all day, and I know what you're doing." Without another word, he turned the golf cart around and drove back down the fairway.

After a second of stunned silence, my foursome looked at each other and shared a hearty laugh. It loosened me up. Leave it to Clyde to come up with something like that.

Apparently, the words *Roly* and *Respect* are not destined to be used in combination. But the ego-bruising regard of my friends has had a curiously perverse effect on me. I've earned it, and I thoroughly enjoy every moment of it. Like senior golf, it's a great thing. The camaraderie, competition, and ego-crushing have kept us young at heart. The common thread is that we're all in various stages of the Ballzheimer's malady. It's twilight time. At the 19th hole, after the round, we now ask for a glass of Geritol instead of the traditional drink.

Some lie!

In the main, golf is a great game played by honorable people. The integrity of the game is based on all the correct things we were taught as children. Follow the rules. Tell the truth. Be honest. Own up to your mistakes and errors. Don't cheat. Have respect and courtesy for others. Sportsmanship and how you play the game are more important than winning.

Unfortunately, there are people who take exception to the rules. And there are bozos who outright cheat. Notice that I call them clowns; that's because they are not golfers and I regard them as lower than what's under a divot.

We've all witnessed one of these clowns thrashing through the woods. He sets the birds to fluttering, trying to escape with their little feathers intact, while small animals flee in all directions, as if from a brush fire. After a three-swing defoliation process, Bozo finally gets to the green, knocks his putt three feet past the hole, and rakes it back to himself. The rake-back represents the consummate gimme.

The answer to the question, "What did you have?" is "Five!!!", usually uttered positively and forcefully. That means this guy knocked down five trees or he orphaned two rabbits and sent three squirrels into psychiatric rehab. Forget the three-foot gimme. Yeah, Bozo, let's get your CPA to audit and sign your card. You already told me how your ball didn't really go out of bounds on the preceding hole. You found it, even though we all watched it hit the condo on the other side of the white stakes.

I don't like to play with these clowns; I'm a shade too outspoken to endure their baloney. Mostly, the cheaters cause problems and resentment. Occasionally, they get theirs, and it makes for some great funny stories.

One such backfire moment was engineered by two golf professionals who were friends of mine. They were part of a weekly skins game. Three or four foursomes participated each week, and the participants were designated as A, B or C players. Handicaps, so important to a wing-ding like this, were kept in an orange book, constantly updated, and strictly observed so that the make-up of the teams was balanced fairly. However, handicap was not used to determine skins (wins) which had to be won at scratch.

It was a fun thing involving moderate, friendly gambling and ending with a few toddies in the bar after the game...for everybody except one clown whom we shall call Freddie. Actually, let's call him "Fast Freddie". This guy always asked for a gas cart because they were faster than the electric carts. Freddie was only fair to middling as a player, but he was superior to sensational in other important golf-related activities.

One was math. He was an absolute master of the handicap

accounting system, playing it with Greenspan-like genius. Freddie had the innate sense of when to go for a putt or when to take a dive on a putt that didn't matter. It depended on the status of the hole and of the match and how it would affect his handicap. Let's just say he would have made the Enron accounting department jealous of his manipulative skills with numbers.

Freddie's prowess in higher mathematics paled in comparison to his tracking skills. He was incredible, a human bloodhound, with the heat-seeking, radar-vectoring capability to always find his golf ball. And I mean ALWAYS. He never lost a ball unless it landed in the water, far in the water, in full view of the entire foursome. It took a majority vote to declare the ball lost and gone. Even then, the rest of the foursome watched nervously for some miraculous reappearance of Freddie's ball. It was facetiously rumored that he could part the waters, find his ball, hit the shot, and clamber out of the hazard before the waters reclosed and got him wet.

Another rumor was that he had connections in the pits of the Indianapolis 500. The group swore that Freddie's carts were souped up. He always beat his foursome to the dense jungle area where his ball landed...and he always found his ball before any other cart arrived on the scene.

My two pals, who had both played on the Tour, decided that Fast Freddie had to be slowed down. They arrived early for the Wednesday skins game, got one of the gas carts, and gave the attendant twenty dollars to put the only other gas cart into a "grounded for maintenance" mode. That left Freddie gasless and forced him into a very sluggish electric cart. The sluggishness was because the attendant had been bribed to assign him an electric cart that was uncharged and weak. It was an elaborate ploy to prevent Fast Freddie from bringing his conniving speed into play.

The skins game started. The first four holes went without incident or opportunity. On the fifth hole, finally Freddie sliced his tee shot right to further right and into impenetrable jungle. My pro pals in the gas cart tore down the fairway, over a rise, and into the densely overgrown area where Freddie's ball had disappeared. Lo and behold, they found his ball. Per their deviously devised plan, they picked up Freddie's ball and pocketed it.

Relegated to the speed of a child's tricycle in his sabotaged golf cart, Slow Freddie appeared on the horizon and headed straight for the dense jungle. Meanwhile, the pro pair pretended to search for Freddie's ball, pushing back foliage and creeper vines with their irons. Much to their surprise, Phenomenal Freddie immediately announced that he had found his ball. And he found it in an ideal open spot. Silence.

What to do? Could the two touring pros admit to picking up his ball and putting it in their pocket? Of course not. Golf is a gentlemen's game. They just stood in the deep foliage, mouths open but unspeaking, and watched Freddie whack it out...onto the green...for a routine par. Whenever I think of him, Fast Freddie brings to mind three things: audacity, mysterious crop circles, and UFO sightings.

Another good friend, Bob Fish, relates a similar story that took place at the club where he was the golf pro. It was a similar set-up and a similar skins game, and there was a fair amount of gambling involved. One of the players was M, an extra-sensory type who always managed without fail to find his errant shots. His balls were marked with a distinctive red M.

Even after his entire foursome searched an area exhaustively and futilely, M's balls always appeared, but only to M...miraculously. Some said M stood for "Mine! I found it." Others said M was short for "Miracle find, you mother!"

M's miraculous finds came thick and fast with every round all summer long...until a low-pressure system off the coastline sent the golf course it's calling card...rain and 50 mph winds. Next day, the grounds crew cleaned up. They came in with buckets of balls bearing the distinctive red M.

Bob quietly returned all the balls to their rightful owner. Immediately thereafter, M seemed to lose his extra-sensory powers. There hasn't been a suspicious string of miracles at that club in years.

Now to the schemiest of all the golf schemes. It took place in the San Francisco Bay area, known for its foggy mornings. A city foursome tournament was being held. It was a scramble with a shotgun start to make the fog experience the same for all participants.

Twenty minutes before the simultaneous tee-off on all holes, a player named Donnie informed his group that he had to take a cart and go back to his car in the lower level of the parking lot. He disappeared into the fog for about ten minutes and got back just in time to pick up his cart partner and head out to the 8th hole, the foursome's starting point.

Number 8 was a short par-four with condominium construction going on behind the green. The foursome hit their opening drives down the middle into the fog. At about 130 yards from the fog-bound green, they found the group's best drive and decided to play it. In a scramble event, everyone in the foursome plays from the spot of the best shot, so the team was in ideal position for their second shots. All agreed that they were 130 yards out and that the distance was perfect for an 8-iron.

When it came Donnie's turn to hit, he selected a 6-iron. The other three argued that he was using way too much club. Donnie insisted that he was going to feather it in, then promptly proceeded to nuke the shot in the general direction of the green. It exploded into the fog like a Tiger Woods 2-iron.

They drove their carts by the green and dismounted to find their shots. One ball was short in front, another was over the green in the back, and a third was in the right-hand trap. The fourth ball, Donnie's, was nowhere to be found. Somebody said, "See, Donnie, we told you that was way too much club. You're probably in one of those condos!"

The team decided the short pitch from in front was their best shot, and Donnie said, "I'll chip first and go for it. Somebody pull that pin." A teammate lifted the flag out and shouted excitedly, "Hey, Donnie, your ball is in the hole. It's an eagle, baby!"

Truly, it was a miracle eagle. Choruses of angels sang, rockets roared, confetti rained from the sky. Or was it a miracle? One of the smarter members of the foursome noticed cart tracks near the green ahead of where their two carts were parked. Since they were the first group to play the 8th hole that morning, those tracks must have come from a greenskeeper. The pin-puller had been the only one to walk on the wet, pristine putting surface, but there was another set of footprints leading to and from the hole in the direction of the mystery cart tracks. Was it the greenskeeper putting the flag in or was it a set-up? Had a hoax been charged off as a great stroke of good fortune?

We'll never know. It's still hotly debated in Bay area golfing circles, and Donnie has long since moved away, taking the little trophy and a little cash prize for that scramble with him. The only thing on which everyone agrees is that a six iron is way too much club from 130 yards.

Hazardous waters.

They say that misfortune is an essential element of humor. That's nowhere more true than in golf. The more you play, the more funny things you see. My mind churns through hundreds of funny episodes at the expense of hundreds of funny people.

In golf, the most bizarre things happen when golfers get the angriest. Water seems to be a primary catalyst. Some of the angriest, funniest incidents I've seen have taken place around water hazards. They seem to bring out the worst in golfers and bring on the most hilarious situations. Simply add water to create a world-class meltdown.

It's only fair that I start with myself. In an act of technological kindness, Beverly bought me a Tayor-Made 3-wood called a Tour Burner. It was the first metal wood I ever had. Up to that time, I had played only with persimmon woods and balata golf balls, the classic tools I had grown to trust. Imagine my surprise and delight when I whacked a hot ball with a metal wood. I figured it had to be illegal. What a weapon to bring into play with my pals!

I play with an extremely competitive bunch at our local course. We have a continuing skins game in a gambling format that involves everyone. It was my first round of golf with the new Tour Burner. I didn't really have a legitimate opportunity to use it until the 13th hole, when I hooked my drive left into a grove of menacing trees. My only way out was to hit a cut-shot up over a levee which guarded a water inlet. The inlet was part of the great San Joaquin Delta water system. Although we're 100 miles from the ocean, the water flows back and forth according to the tides. I chose this obstacle and this shot to dazzle my playing partners with my new metal wood for the first time.

Somehow I should have known the club would be the instrument of my meltdown. Later, my pals referred to that cut-shot as "the crappiest shot Roly ever hit." Here's what happened: just as I hit the ball, the Tour Burner caught a limb. The limb struck me in the face, drawing blood. I super-cut the shot. The ball veered away from the delta and kept veering all the way across the fairway. It missed the intended landing area and bounced into the men's room in the maintenance shed. The men's room was known to all of us as "the crap house". Thus, it became "the crappiest shot Roly ever hit," and I have explained the complex combination of events that caused it.

There's more to this meltdown. In an unparalleled act of uncoordinated follow-through, I drew the Tour Burner back to punish it for its crappy performance. I intended to throw it a record distance. As I began my forward launch motion, I became aware that there was a paved maintenance road in front of me. If I released the club at the proper moment, it would land on the pavement. My new metal 3-wood gift from my wife would probably be destroyed or at least horribly defaced. These thoughts of doom flooded my brain in an instant. An angry Bev flashed before my conscience.

The nightmarish vision made me hold on a millisecond too long. The Tour Burner flew up over the levee into the delta canal. The minute the club left my hand, I knew I was in deep doo-doo. I ran to the top of the levee and saw the butt of the grip bobbing on the surface. The tide was going out. I had nothing with which to retrieve the club. Panic set in. This was grounds for divorce. What to do? What to do?

As if by divine intervention, clarity replaced the panic in my mind. The tide was going out, and the gift club was floating ever so slightly in the direction of the clubhouse. Careful calculations had to be made, requiring an elementary knowledge of physics, calculus, tides, and hydraulics. Child's play, considering I was a trained Air Force navigator.

I plotted it in my mind. Finish the hole; check the club's position. Play the next hole; check tidal drift. Finish the round; find the floating grip-end near the clubhouse. Fashion a retriever; use a flagstick with a fishing line loop at the end. Find a helper.

When the round was over, I enlisted the aid of Fluor, one of my skins-game buddies, offering to buy him a beer after we got the Tour Burner. We took a golf cart and sighted the 3-wood butt still barely afloat. My good friend Fluor leaned on the bank of the canal reaching with pole in hand while I anchored him by gripping his other hand. We leaned and stretched, trying to lasso the butt bobbing below us in the murky, moving water. Every time we got close, the tide would push the club just out of our reach. With cunning mathematical precision, we positioned ourselves slightly ahead of the anticipated drift. Finally the club bobbed in our direction, but it remained tantalizingly just out of reach. We stretched, groaned, reached, moaned, all to no avail. Fluor was extended at an angle of 45 degrees to the water, and it still wasn't enough.

To this day, I can't explain my next act, and I truly regret it. I let go of Fluor. He splashed head-first into the canal. When he stood up, the water was up to his neck. Dripping sea weed decorated his head. I couldn't resist. I said softly with a quavering apologetic smile, "Hey, Fluor, I'm sorry. While you're in there, would you be good enough to grab my club."

The ride back was made in silence. There was no mention of beer. In fact, for several years there was no conversation between us. I still feel badly. Fluor, if you read this, buddy, thanks a lot. Can I buy you that beer?

While I was in the Air Force at Mather, we played weekend fun tournaments. We usually had twenty to forty players, ranging in rank from airmen to full colonels. The group generally included a couple of former state champions, the local club professional, and an airman called "Mikie", who had been a runner-up in the U.S. Junior Championship. Although he had a little hitch in his personality profile, Mikie was a good guy, and we enjoyed his game and his company.

Assigned to duty at the base golf course because of his abilities, Mikie was an exceptional player. He had a sound swing, great rhythm, and a good grasp of all aspects of the game, except one. You might say Mikie lacked the proper temperament. He was emotional and excitable. In short, he had a helluva temper. Mikie once threw a club on the driving range...because he couldn't get the wind to stop blowing.

Many of us had tempers, and we all occasionally threw clubs or tantrums in reaction to a bad shot or a bad break. As with all wild things, control was imposed on us. The senior officers in our group strongly requested that we hold back on the emotional theatrics. It was decided that, if anyone heaved a club, the offender would have to buy beer for all the other participants. Even at military rates back in those days, it amounted to at least a ten-dollar fine. That was a lot of money to Mikie.

In the first round after the mandate, Mikie was having an uncharacteristically bad day. His characteristic means of venting anger had been banned, and the pressure of the no-throw rule weighed heavily upon him. His game, his day, and his self-control got worse as he went along. Occasionally, a goading "Throw it!" was heard.

On the par-three 11th hole, he hit a perfect 8-iron over a lake, 140 yards to a flag placement dangerously near the front of the green. His ball landed about eight feet past the hole. The backspin took it back toward the hole for a possible hole-in-one. As the ball traveled, the backspin seemed to increase. The ball spun past the hole, narrowly missed going in, spun off the green, trickled down an incline, and plopped softly into the water.

Could any of us tolerate such injustice? Mikie cocked the 8-iron in his right hand. Shouts of "Throw it!" resounded around him. We waited for the sight of the club sailing against the blue sky, bringing us the best-tasting beer of the day. It didn't happen.

Torn by indecision, stricken by thoughts of the ten-dollar beer fine, Mikie's shoulders sagged as he dropped the offending 8-iron to the turf and raised his eyes to heaven. Suddenly, his spirit resurged; you could see the anger resurface as he braced himself on his right leg and ripped off his left golf shoe. He walked unevenly to the lake, fired the Footjoy straight into the water, and pumped his fists.

He had overcome the mandate and the system. Throwing the golf shoe had never been discussed, and there was no local shoe rule to be invoked. In over a half-century of golf, I have never witnessed such a triumph of creative anger. Mikie finished the round shoeless. The second Footjoy followed another unrewarded shot into the water; it was not as spectacular as the first shoe. After the round, we bought the beers for Mikie. It was our salute to mind over matter.

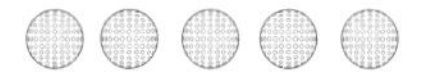

When it comes to the classics, I have a favorite meltdown. Again, it occurred at Mather and involved the bandits I played golf with in my “Air Farce” days. The perpetrator was a guy named Harley, who was the son of a retired officer. In way of introduction, Harley was infamous for habitually breaking his putter on the 18th green. He snapped one nearly every round, and his little Volkswagen bug held almost 100 broken putter shafts in its front trunk.

One day, as Harley left the golf course, he ran into the back end of an unmoving Air Force dumptruck. It made quite a scene: the big blue truck with the little VW bug smashed under the big blue dump bin...with broken putter heads and shafts strewn all over the road.

The Air Police arrived at the accident scene with lights flashing. Before they could ask, Harley informed them that the truck had stopped abruptly for no apparent reason and that the driver had fled on foot. He added that the driver should be captured and courtmartialed.

The Air Police sergeant snorted and retorted, “Nice try, Sonny. This dumptruck hasn’t moved for three days. It’s been parked here because it has transmission problems.” Harley was lucky they didn’t charge him with running some kind of illegal operation in shattered putters.

All this is only an introduction to Harley. Now to his classic meltdown which took place during a two-man team tournament at a Sacramento golf course.

Harley was playing under duress. He hated tournaments because they "stifled his artistic emotionalism." In other words, he had to keep his infamous temper moderately under control.

Harley and his partner, Artie, were going along nicely. The match was even until the 13th hole. There, Harley went after a ten-foot birdie putt too strongly, went way past the cup, and ended up three-putting. That put his team one-down and started a wee bit of anger percolating in Harley's head.

The 14th hole was a little par-three fronted by a shallow lake and guarded by bunkers. Both men on the opposing team hit their shots safely onto the green, but not particularly close to the hole. Artie hit third and buried his ball under the lip of the front bunker.

It was Harley's turn. He threw his ball down, didn't bother with a tee or much of an address, and proceeded to hit a fat 7-iron into the middle of the lake. As if it was an intrinsic part of his follow-through, Harley sailed his 7-iron into the lake toward the spreading ripples. Without stopping his motion, he grabbed his bag and strode directly toward the flag, straight into the lake. Walking purposefully through the water, even as it rose above his waist and neared his neck, he reached the area where the 7-iron had landed. He bent over, put his face in the water, submerged briefly, and reappeared with wet weeds on his head and the 7-iron in his dripping fist. He continued on his course all the way across the lake and came out of the water some 90 yards later.

It was a soggy sight that will long live in the memory of all who witnessed it. There was a gallery of about fifty onlookers.

They were absolutely flabbergasted. For Harley, it was just another day at the office. Later in the day, Artie was surrounded by a group of curious and amused tournament attendees who wanted to know all about the bizarre incident. Someone asked, "Weren't you afraid he might drown?"

"Hell, no," Harley's partner answered. "He couldn't keep his head down over a shot all day long, and I knew he wouldn't keep it down in that lake either!"

Fairways full of crazy characters.

Throughout a lifetime in golf, I have met a gallery of offbeat and downright zany characters and have enjoyed them all. My picks for outstanding characters were made from literally hundreds of funny, crazy golfers. I present for your entertainment the cream of the crop.

To my mind, the most memorable was a guy named Vern Callison, nicknamed P.O.V. (Poor Old Vern). Unfortunately, he now resides on the wrong side of the grass, but Vern was one of the great amateurs in the United States. He had won just about every major tournament in northern California, and he was the California State Amateur Champion in 1959 and 1965, winning by large margins. For good measure, he won the USGA Publinx Championship twice and was the oldest man to win that title. You know he could play. He was a rare gem blessed with incredible golfing ability, but that was just one facet of the man.

His looks made most people smile. He was balding with a little pot belly and always had a big grin on his face. It was an ultimate honor to be included in his circle of friends, and that held true for golfers and non-golfers alike.

Everyone in golf knew Vern Callison, and those who didn't said they did. Even now, someone will ask, "Tell us a Vern Callison story." The tales are always funny and outlandish...and true. I often think I'm invited to certain events not because of my playing ability, but because of my wealth of Callison stories.

His license plates were the first vanity plates I'd ever seen: POV. He called everyone he especially liked "Gate"; I have no idea why. His wobbly walk resembled a fighter faking his own imminent knock-out. Vern always looked like he was on his last legs, but the man was a fox. He never talked about himself or his abilities in anything but self-deprecating terms and always for the sake of humor.

For most of his life, Vern was a bachelor, but that didn't stop him from being active with the ladies. His roommates on golf trips had to be on the alert for the sock on the door handle, a signal device that meant Vern had company. Many times, I've had to go back and sit through a movie for the second or third viewing while I waited for Vern's sock to drop.

Everybody loved the guy, and he joked with everybody. When he focused his practical-joking expertise on you, it would take two days to figure out that he'd given you "a gotcha". Playing a joke on you was the highest form of being in with Vern.

His funny golf swing led many opponents to say there was no way he could beat them. Famous last words. Standing over the golf ball, he looked like an unmade bed. Most of the time, that unmade bed was his opponents' undoing. Even when Vern became an aging senior, it was a rarity for anyone to beat him.

All the older touring pros knew Vern. He was the guy who could have made it on the Tour if he wanted to. But, as much as he loved golf, he enjoyed enjoying life more. Vern's participation in a golf tournament gave the event immediate credibility. He had charisma, and like Arnold Palmer, the gallery always gravitated to him.

Vern was a *bon vivant*, code word for one who savors more than an occasional cocktail. In happy coincidence, he owned and ran a watering hole in Sacramento. It goes without saying that I knew him well. Vern seldom worked at his tavern. His dad ran the place. Vern's primary function was to grab last night's receipts and be off on a golf trip, leaving the bookkeeper to pull out his hair as he tried to reconcile the till and the register tapes.

My nickname, the Frog, was given to me by Vern. He dubbed me that while we were playing in our customary foursome, composed of Vern, Tom Dixon, Mel Hutchins and myself. These guys all could play. Tom Dixon was the San Francisco City Golf Champ. Mel Hutchins, a low handicapper, had been a forward for the Fort Wayne Pistons and an NBA all-star. He was a big man and could really rip a golf ball. In the match on my christening day, Mel hit a huge drive, and I managed to stay up with him. Vern exclaimed, "Mel, we've got the little Frog jumping today." The nickname stayed with me...to this day.

Vern was so taken with his deprecating nickname for me that it inspired him to other creative acts. One day, he came into the coffee shop at Hoffman Park, where I was the assistant pro and leading coffee-consumer, and yelled, "Frog! Somebody just stole your new golf bag."

The S.O.B.s! This was a beautiful white leather tour bag, illegally consigned to me by a prestigious golf club manufacturer. It was my pride and joy. I ran outside and found the bag missing. However, my clubs were neatly laid on the ground next to my watch, rings, wallet, and other contents in a tidy pile. Something smelled suspicious.

"P.O.V., when someone steals a bag, they don't usually leave all the contents in a neat pile," I said accusatively.

"Right, Froggy, you're a smart little Frog," he rejoined. "Just trust Poor Old Vern, and you'll have your bag back in a week."

I had no choice; the bag was gone. One week later, it showed up, but without my name and with the clubmaker affiliation removed. In their place on the pristine white leather was painted in full color a giant cartoon bullfrog, sitting on a golf ball. The name that blazed next to it was LE FROG. I found out later that this joke cost Vern more than $100. In 1968, it was a pretty expensive practical joke. That Vern, he was somethin' else.

Later that year, same foursome, Vern and Mel engaged in an uncharacteristically adult conversation. It was rumored that Bon Vivant Vern was in the throes of some very serious partying. Mel, a straight-and-narrow Mormon, was questioning Vern's after-hours activities.

"P.O.V., we've got the two-man tournament coming up soon, and you're horribly out of shape," said Mel, who always stayed in great shape. Vern protested profusely, claiming he was in the peak of condition.

Mel took it further: "P.O.V., I heard that you were out until 4:00 AM last Friday and you never even came home Saturday night." Again, Vern protested that he was the victim of scurrilous slander, highly exaggerated rumors at best.

Finally, Mel dispelled the double-talk when he asked, "Vern, what exactly have you been doing to get yourself in some kind of shape for the tournament?"

"Well, Mel," replied Vern, "just last night I slept with the window open!"

Vern, the world-class athlete. He was a breath of fresh air. We became great pals, but I had to constantly keep an eye on him. He confided in me, and I, proud to be his confidant, inevitably found out later that he had made me the goat of some complex joke. He was so gifted and intelligent at his craft that it took me days and sometimes weeks to figure out that the joke was on me. Never malicious, always funny, it was just his way, because he liked me.

One day, as I was driving past his business, Callison's Tavern, I heard a yell. "Frog! Stop and come over here!" I made a U-turn and went back to Vern's place. "I've got something to show you, and I'm sort of embarrassed about it," he told me.

Not knowing what to expect, I asked, "What's up, P.O.V.?"

"You know that golf club company named Shamrock?" Vern answered. "Well, they sent me a golf bag with my name on it. That embarrasses me." Vern never liked to flaunt his golfing success.

"Hey, are you going to show the bag to me or not?"

"Okay," said Vern, "but remember I didn't ask for this." He opened his car's trunk, and there was a beautiful white golf bag, just like mine, with his name on it. It was surrounded by a dozen bottles of booze, all full. As he pulled the bag out to show it to me, a bottle of brandy came with it, tumbled out, and hit the pavement, exploding into a shower of liquor and glass.

"P.O.V., you've got an entire cocktail lounge right there in your trunk! What the hell are you doing?"

Vern studied me seriously and said, "Frog, you know I've got to lose weight and you know I like a little drink now and then. I figured if I could find some liquor that tastes terrible, then I wouldn't be tempted to drink." He paused and grinned. "But, Frog, you know what? I like it all!" That was the end of Vern's Weight Watchers special.

Everything else aside, Vern was a gentleman, especially on the golf course. He was a gracious winner and a wonderful loser when he occasionally lost. One of my fondest remembrances of him was our club championship in 1975. I was still considered a professional, but Vern lobbied the club to allow me to compete. Fate put Vern and me in the 36-hole final.

On that day, we played 16 holes dead even, then I won 17 and birdied 18 to go two up. When we finished the first 18, Vern asked, "Frog, do you need lunch or can we start the second 18 without it?" It was fine with me to skip lunch; I was pumped. I birdied the next four holes to go six up on my pal, the perennial champion, a legend of golf.

On the par-three 5th, I hit my shot about 20 feet from the hole. Vern stuck his within one foot. We started for the hole, Vern in his cart and I walking, and got to the green at the same time. I was aided by the adrenaline pumping over my socks and into my shoes. Going first, I knocked my putt in for my sixth straight bird and hit Vern's ball away for a gimme.

On air, I galloped to the 6th tee and proceeded to smoke my drive. Vern barely arrived in time to see the ball scream down the fairway and come to rest almost 300 yards away. Vern stood over his tee shot, bald head bobbing, pot belly bouncing (he claimed it turned to muscle on the downswing), wiggling his waggle, and abruptly stopped.

"Frog, are you double-parked somewhere?" For the only time I know of, Vern started laughing at his own cheap shot, and he lost it. I remember it took a full two minutes for him to regain his composure enough to hit his drive.

We walked down the sixth fairway with our hands on each other's shoulders. A friend drove Vern's cart while we laughed and enjoyed one of the great moments of our friendship. P.O.V. is gone, but not forgotten. He was absolutely one of a kind.

Irv Green, another friend of mine, was a great golfer...only in his own mind. We took off from work one day and played nine holes at the local course. On the last hole, Irv sliced his drive into the trees on the right side and tried to rescue himself with a great trouble shot ala Arnold Palmer. Unfortunately, he wasn't as gifted as Arnie and the shot ricocheted off several trees. Not one to give up easily, Irv tried again...and again...and again...all with the same tree-knocking results. After approximately seven unsuccessful attempts, he looked at me imploringly. I was busily raising one arm over my head and dropping it to my side, then repeating the motion with the other arm, and so on.

Irv couldn't stand it and bellowed, "What the hell are you doing? Can't you see I'm in trouble here?"

"I figured you were taking batting practice," I answered. "And since this has turned into a baseball game, I'm giving you The Wave, except this is a one-man wave."

Irv's response was not suitable for disclosure in this or any other printed publication.

Irv is the same guy who decided he wanted to caddy for me in the State Amateur at Pebble Beach. My first assigned course was Spyglass Hill, ever-popular for its difficulty. I had an old PGA tour-book used by the pros for the Bing Crosby annual event. It was an early version of the current yardage books.

On the 1st hole at Spyglass, a par-five, I was at the bottom of the hill in two. I took a look at my yardage book, counted my paces to the three green irrigation covers, consulted the pin-placement chart provided by the California Golf Association and factored in the pin placement, then added yards for the off-shore winds coming directly at us.

I said to Irv, "Let's see, that's 10 paces added to 111 yrds, with the pin 22 yards back, and another 10 yards for the wind. I make it 143 yards." Irv just stood there by the bag with a silly grin on his face while I was doing my compilations. "Let me have the 7-iron," I concluded, "or don't you think that's enough?" Irv didn't move, didn't say anything, so I said, "Well?"

Finally Irv spoke: "You know, Frog, I just figured something out. Not only am I not good enough to play in this tournament, I'm not even smart enough to do the math!" But Irv was smart enough not to caddy for me again. He knew his limitations.

Jose Santiago was one of the most entertaining characters I've ever had the pleasure to be around. Jose was the head pro at the Stockton municipal course for a quarter of a century, and it was a humorous twenty-five years. The course was located in the low-income part of town. It demanded a pro with the necessary conjones to rule the roost. Jose was the man.

My first encounter with him took place on that course, approximately 1,000 yards from the pro shop. I was playing with Ernie Godina, whom I had known for ten years as a regular member of our skins game. Ernie had just relocated to become Jose's assistant, and the skins game followed him. We were putting on the 7th green, geographically in the middle of the course, when I first heard Jose's voice. It came over the pro shop loudspeaker like the thunderous voice of The Almighty from heaven.

"You gonna play golf or should I send out a picnic lunch?!!"

It startled me, and I asked Ernie, "Who and what the hell is that?"

Ernie shrugged and said, "That's Jose."

I responded, "Well, it sounded like God."

"That is God," Ernie said. "He is Jose."

At that moment, I knew I was in Jose Country.

Over the next few years, Jose and I became fast friends. Everybody knew Jose, knew he was the man in charge, and had a story about him. He worked seven days a week. Except for golf junkets with the members or occasional family vacations, Jose was there every day and opened the pro shop every morning.

One morning, Jose arrived at the appointed time, a half-hour before sunrise. Naturally, it was still dark. One of the crankier members was already standing by the door, obviously impatient for Jose to show up. As Jose put his key in the lock, Mr. Impatient commented, "You're a little late, aren't you, pro?"

Jose, who could be a man of few words when the situation warranted, quietly withdrew his key and walked over to the coffee shop. For the next half-hour, he read the paper and sipped his coffee. He then went back to the pro shop where the early-bird was still waiting. Jose put his key in the door and asked, "Am I on time for you now?" The chastened jerk knew better than to say anything. Jose announced, "The course is now open."

Normally, Jose took good care of his customers and was fair to everyone. Our skins game participants always had tee times, and we were there every weekend, rain or shine. We were the core of the men's club and the backbone of support for the city course. However, we never received any special favors.

It happened that I was practice-chipping to a green with a sign that read NO CHIPPING when I heard the voice of Jose on the P.A. system: "Hey, Frog! Be careful. One of those chips might hit that sign and bounce off and hit you in the eye!" That was the diplomatic Jose.

Once I asked him why we didn't have a member-guest golf day. He responded in typical Jose fashion, "Why? Because if the local jail had a lock-down, we'd lose half of our members." That brought a smile for the truth in it.

The shop and starter's desk were run with an iron hand, and he had a good system. You didn't pay your greens fees until you were called in to pay. The Lord help you if you tried to break that rule. If a stranger came in to get on the waiting list, he was informed of that policy and told when he would tee off. God help you if you came in early to bother Jose.

One unsuspecting golfer didn't follow procedure. He not only kept trying to bag Jose, he also dared to ask if their group had enough time to visit the nearest sporting goods store to buy some golf balls.

RED ALERT! RED ALERT!

Jose calmly picked up the waiting list, crumpled it into a tight wad, threw it into the wastebasket, and said, “Yeah, you have plenty of time. While you’re there, get on their waiting list.” Group deleted.

Jose took no prisoners. When he retired, he was roasted by his friends at the dinner. Well done. It was a fitting end to a wonderfully tempestuous career.

Golfers from every socio-economic class make my crazy characters list. Pat Bennett retired young and decided he would make himself a low-handicapper. Pat was a financial guru for many companies and became very successful. He was a CFO and a shareholder in most of the ventures, putting his money where his mouth was. Well-educated, with an extensive accounting and business background, he considered any business problem something he could ultimately solve. His success came from his intelligence, experience, diligence, and tenacity. You get the idea; he was dedicated to getting the job done and doing it right.

When his country club was about to be sold against the wishes of the members, he orchestrated the purchase of the club by the members. This was while the economy wasn’t flourishing and there was a glut of golf clubs in the area.

That was the good news. The bad news is that he went after

golf with the same qualities and tenacity he had employed in business. This former CFO tried to bull his way to a better game, and it better yield to him, by God! Pat certainly wouldn't give up. He wanted to be a player, and he sought to perfect his swing. With total concentration and preparation, he went about the task. Goals were formulated; excellent instruction was purchased and worked at diligently; practice sessions were highly structured. His pre-shot routine was without parallel. One could rearrange the patio furniture in the time it took him to go through his pre-shot ritual.

Practice swing beside the ball. Two-perspective visualization of intended flight. Then a plumb-bob-like aiming procedure that was classified information, available only on a Need-to-Know basis. Another practice swing down the line from behind the ball. In conclusion, worthy of a Viet Cong ambusher, a sneak-up maneuver to the address position. And he's ready. A few dance steps, the final head-bob, and he triggers his swing...resulting in an otherwise unimpressive hit.

Incidentally, apart from his grinding approach to the game, Pat had a great sense of humor, loved to swap insults, and was a genuinely compassionate man. He was going to need all that, especially his sense of humor.

Pat was the anchor man for a scramble team in a tournament at his club. They came to the 7th hole doing well, largely because of Pat's play. Their tee shot, however, was in deep rough, and each of the other three team members had tried unsuccessfully to get it out in good position.

It was Pat's turn. He started his pre-shot routine: practice swing, visualization, top-secret aiming procedure, final practice swing, etc. Meanwhile, the members' clothing went out of style and play backed up for three holes. But it was all right; it was a crucial shot. He got to address, did the dance steps and stopped. When he looked down there was no ball! He had totally forgotten to put his ball down after his predecessor had hit from the same spot.

Pat had flamed out in mid-air, with great embarrassment and loss of image. I have since explained to him the various manifestations of Ballzheimer's, though I would have thought him too young and focused for the disease.

With golf characters, I often see things I have never seen before in fifty years of playing. Howie was an average golfer who became addicted to the game. And Howie hated depositing new golf balls into the same old water hazards. In fact, it really ticked him off to unintentionally wash a premium $4.00 ball and not get it back.

On the 16th at Brookside C.C., there are two lakes to avoid. Having already hooked his tee shot into the first lake, Howard was extremely upset when his fourth shot hit the green and backspun off into the second lake. He placed his bag with its two stand-up legs near the edge of the water and walked along the bank, trying to locate his ball for recovery. He glanced back to see his bag totter toward the water. The legs had given way to the fluffy bank grass, and the tilt worsened in slow-motion.

Howie stood paralyzed. He was too far away to save his equipment from a bath. He did the only thing he could think of...he screamed, "Bite!" It didn't help. The bag went down and the clubs poured out into the lake. Oh, the irony. Bags do not bite!

There are many such stories and many, many more crazy characters in my bag of memories. These few prompt me to remember a fairway full of others, but tha-tha-that's all for now, folks.

I'm holding up play. We have to move along to the 17th.

Gamesmanship: knees and needles.

I greatly enjoy two things that I connect with golf. Neither one is in the rule book, but both have become an essential part of the game for me. The first is *playing for knee*, something I started with and for my friends. The second is *needling*, the wonderful insults, put-downs, and zingers that seem to flow naturally during a round with pals.

The average golfer may never experience anything like the touring professionals do when they win. Chances are there won't be many occasions to sip champagne from a silver cup or raise a crystal trophy above your head or hear the cheers of the gallery for an exceptional shot. That acclaim is for those who are among the best in the game.

However, golf can reward you with something unique and personal... a moment and a prize that even elite professionals don't have. Playing for knee can provide your reward, your trophy, your ultimate satisfaction derived from the game of golf. And just what is playing for knee?

Playing for knee is playing for the bragging rights of a long-term rivalry. In sports, there are many such rivalries between individuals and teams. Think tennis and you think of Connors vs

McEnroe. Think baseball, and it's the Yankees vs Red Sox. How about the San Francisco 49ers vs the Oakland Raiders?

Bragging rights are always an issue. Not a big deal, according to the losers. People say that a few years down the road no one will remember who finished second. That's a bunch of baloney! The ones who finished second will always remember not winning. And the winners will always remember who they beat. Those moments are indelibly etched into heart and brain. When in later life you meet your opponent, a strange thing happens: you both remember who won...and who didn't.

You undoubtedly have a pal with whom you regularly play golf. Every week this guy kicks your butt on the golf course because he's better at the game...started at a younger age...has more time to practice...doesn't have to worry about all the things you do...has all the latest high-tech equipment...has better leverage because he's taller...whatever. Let's just say he has your number. In fact, he has his bank deposit slips preprinted with your check routing number to make it easier to bank his winnings. Your losses are an integral part of his income, and he makes a good living from taking your money while pounding your pride. In fact, he knows he's got you. He counts his chickens before the first shot is hit. But it isn't the money that bothers you; it's the audacity of the guy and the humiliation you feel from being his patsy.

If just once you could turn the tables, beat him at his own game, thrash and trash him the way he does you. How many times have you wished that?!

As it always does, the worm turns. Inevitably, if you don't give up and work hard and live right, your day comes. You're all over the guy who usually beats you. Hole after hole, you hold on. Coming into the eighteenth, you're still on top. You stick the clinching shot right by the flag. You knock in a five-footer for the win! The feeling of victory is intense.

As my golf buddy, Bob Fish, puts it: "I can't hear your congratulations because they are drowned out by a chorus of angels singing Hallelujah!" I always think of it as the same feeling a kid gets when he legitimately beats his father at a game the kid has never won before.

Now your playing partner, this friend from Hell whom you've finally beaten, the recent former bane of your existence, kneels down in front of you on the eighteenth green, before God and the other two guys in your foursome...and, hopefully, some spectators and the people on the clubhouse porch...and declares: "It has been a pleasure to get my butt kicked by such a wonderful person and fine golfer as you."

That is playing for knee. It's like everything else in life. You have the opportunity to win or you can lose. If you lose, you have to face the consequences. You can be humbled and humiliated or you can be a glorious winner. The choice is yours.

Playing for knee gives you a great reason to keep trying, to work on improving your game, to practice humility, and to properly enjoy winning. I make it a point to introduce the concept of playing for knee to new golfing friends. My friends, new and old, seem to relish the idea of beating a former wise-guy pro and humiliating me in public. On the other hand, I enjoy the pressure it puts on me to keep this from happening. I find it makes me focus and play better, and it hypes my enjoyment of the round. We all come out way ahead.

Just as in a doctor's office, sticking someone with a needle is an art form. The best just might be when the persons on the receiving end don't realize they've been jabbed.

We've all had a laugh from the classic golf put downs. After a weak drive, someone will say, "Does your husband play golf?" or "I think you broke your bra strap on that one!" When a member of the foursome skulls a terrible shot that somehow ends up near the pin, you'll inevitably hear the shortest, most sarcastic insult in golf: "Nice Shot!"

I got a glimpse of the sardonic side of golf when I was about 14 years old. After finishing a round in a Junior golf tournament, I sat down at a table in the club snack shop and found myself face to face with two of professional basketball's greatest players: Bill Russell and Bill Sharman of the Boston Celtics. They were NBA champions and sports gods in the Boston area, and they were just across the table, waiting for the Juniors to clear out so they could play.

I gulped and chirped, "Are you who I think you are?"

With a twinkle in his eye, Russell asked back, "Who do you think we are?" At nearly seven feet in height, with a face recognized internationally, he was hard to mistake.

"You're the Celtics!" I shot right back. No flies on me. I could hold my own with one of sport's most famous needlers and trash-talkers.

I knew that Bill Sharman had just retired from basketball and was starting a new career in professional golf. He was an assistant pro at a club somewhere in the area. I grabbed this opportunity to talk to him, golfer to golfer, by asking, "Mr. Sharman, which sport do you think is tougher to play, basketball or golf?"

He thought it over for a moment and answered, "In basketball, when I get the ball, I dribble, shoot or pass. I do it all on instinct without thinking. In golf, I hit a shot, then I have a few minutes to think about my next one. A round takes four and one-half hours with only about 20 minutes of hitting, so there's time for a lot of other stuff to take place. That time between shots can make it nerve-wracking, so I think that golf is tougher for me."

I knew what he meant. "Other stuff" takes place in all sports. The object is to psych out your opponent. On the basketball floor or the football field, the time between plays leaves time for psychological warfare. That "other stuff" becomes trash talk, insults designed to get the opponents' goat.

However, in the genteel sport of golf, it translates into the gentle art of needling and is employed at a higher, more gentlemanly level. Hollering "Miss!" in the middle of someone's backswing is not considered correct form. Golfers practice a more refined, intellectual approach to this art. And, as in any other art form, the practitioners of needling have varying skill levels. Trash becomes treasure for the players who are masters of needling. They are insidious and subtle, and their needling comes in many forms.

Some of my friends utilize the personal insult in their techniques. It can be subtle or not so subtle. I have been told that I am one of the finest practitioners of the insult in my weight class. I take it as a compliment, considering the heavyweights I associate with. Some in my skins group constantly search for pigeons with fast backswings and fat wallets, and they heap abuse on the poor patsies while they take their money. Talk about moral degradation!

I have some favorites from my vast collection of needles, and my preference is generally for the subtle and insidious. My friend, Bob Fish, knows how to disengage my gears, usually with humor. Sometimes it doesn't work. One day during America's war with Iraq, as my 3-iron to a long par three popped out of a trap, he asked, "Do you know why you bounced out of that trap, Froggy?"

I said, "No. I give up, Fish. Why did I bounce out?"

"The French don't like sand," he replied.

I got it; the reference was to France's reluctance to join in the war. Pretty intellectual, hey? Fish thought the remark might get into my head and influence my play. He forgot that I'm not intellectual at all. And I'm an American Frog.

One person in our group pretends to be a connoisseur of landscapes and topography. As we play, he makes it a point to demonstrate his appreciation of the beauty of every lake, stream, and well-formed grove of trees. As he extols the beauty all around us, he also reminds us how close those beautiful objects are to the line of flight of our intended shots. All of nature's wonders were put on the golf course just to supply this guy with ammunition for his needle-gun.

His psych goes something like this: "I can hit it over that lake...usually...but it will be easier for you; you're longer than I am." How's that for some subtle pre-shot messing with the mind?

Many years ago, before my quick turn at the PGA Tour, I was playing amateur golf in Sacramento. One of my regular opponents was Hal Ingram, a golf professional of considerable talent. Hal was a very long knocker, and that was his claim to fame. One day, Hal and I were playing with Vern Callison, the Pavarotti of needlers. Ingram had just creamed his drive. I nailed mine and was right next to him.

With a suggestive wink, Vern whispered so only I could hear, "Just play along with me." Then Vern commented, "You almost caught that one, huh, Frog."

"Yeah, just a little off center," I replied.

For the rest of the round, Hal made sure that I would never outdrive him again. You could almost hear his thinking process: to hell with the bet; no Frog is going to outdrive me. Needless to say, it cost him the match. Vern, with a big grin, just watched Hal do himself in. When it was over, we all had a good laugh about it, including the sheepish, recently-sheared Ingram.

Vern was a master, but insidious compliments are part of my game bag, too. My favorite is: "Great shot...for that type of swing." Usually, that brings a smile from two playing partners and a cold stare from the wounded shotmaker. Hey, I just wanted to compliment the guy.

Another of my golf pals is a retired college professor named Dick Park, who could write an authoritive book on the art of needling. Dick's golf swing has mystified and terrorized at least eleven teaching pros. The clubhead travels in so many different directions that the Automobile Association of America has cancelled his membership while he was playing. I'm proud to say that I got this great needler with the kind of remark he'd use himself. He hit a particularly good shot, and I said to him, "Nice shot, Dick. I know no one will ever tell you nice swing."

Every so often, tried and trusted needles lose their impact and go out of style. How many times have you heard: "Nice hit, Alice." or "Sweet swing, Sweetie." The inference is that the guy hits it like a girl. However, since Annika Sorenstam came on the scene and held her own with the men, that needle isn't too sharp anymore. I know a thousand guys who'd like to hit it like Annika does. Or like any of the talented ladies on the LPGA Tour.

One of the classic needles was given in complete silence. I learned about it from Poor Old Vern. Years ago, he was pitted against a college phenom in the California State Fair golf tournament. Vern was already a grizzled veteran. His opponent was Al Geiberger, a Sacramento native who ultimately became a great on the Tour and the first man to ever shoot a 59 in PGA competition.

A gallery of more than one thousand spectators followed them as they stayed within striking range of each other during the entire championship match. On the 16th green, Geiberger was away and unveiled his innovative method of plumb-bobbing to determine the line of his putt. For the uninitiated, plumb-bobbing is a procedure whereby the player putting stands behind the ball and lines it up in a straight line to the hole. Then the player suspends the putter with the shaft vertically at eye level, closes one eye, and blocks out the ball. The shaft position, right or left of the hole, tells the player how much break to estimate. Almost no one was familiar with the technique. At the time, it was as startling an innovation as today's titanium clubheads.

The gallery was transfixed as Geiberger dangled his putter and squinted down the line. None of them had seen anything like this. Vern just watched, taking it all in. Geiberger knocked in a curling 20-footer, and the gallery went wild.

Blank-faced, Vern stood behind his 15-footer, raised his putter, and did the opposite of his opponent. He held the putter parallel to the ground, not vertical. Vern had no idea what he was doing, but he put on a masterful performance. He peered over the parallel shaft from the grip, then from the putter head. He went through enough gyrations to qualify as a flight controller signalling landing instructions to incoming pilots on a carrier deck. And he did it all in mock seriousness without a word.

The gallery was buzzing and tittering, and everyone watched intently with a collective silly grin. Not Vern; he grew deadly serious. He stood over the putt and drilled it dead-center into the hole. Amid cheers and applause, Vern shrugged and ambled off the green. I can't remember who won, but Poor Old Vern will always be remembered for one of the greatest silent needles of all time.

Another of my skins-game buddies, Bobby Goleman, is a superb needler and a heck of a player. Bobby is a pigtailed, pot-bellied piece of work with a rockabilly accent. He loves to laugh and usually has plenty of funny ammunition for his needle-gun. He's also fond of betting with everybody on the course. Win or lose, he's a lot of fun and a terrific competitor.

Bobby wrote a poem about putting, and it gives his view of the golf game. It isn't really a specific needle, but in a general regard, it is.

Ode to My Putter

Ah, there's my driver that I swing with such might.
Sometimes it goes straight, but then left and then right.

My long irons, you see, are a devilish crew, too;
If not hit perfectly, the ball goes askew.

The mid-irons are easier, but still hard to hit.
If you don't get the sweet spot, they give you a fit.

The short irons and wedges, these are my friends.

Mishit them a little, and they still find the pins.

Now comes the putter, it's my most trusted club.
If I screw up the others, it will pick me back up.

When the round's on the line and I need this last putt,
a tough downhiller, I feel it in my gut.

When I stroke this last putt and I watch it go in,
I daze my opponents with a smirkish grin.

Just me and my putter, my most trusted friend.

I will conclude with a funny zinger where I was on the receiving end. Again, it's an oblique needle, and it's directed at neurotics who take golf lessons.

I was playing poorly in the San Francisco City Amateur, but managed to get through my first few matches. Apprehensive about my upcoming match, I walked into the pro shop and asked if the teaching pro could take a look at my swing for half an hour. Yes was the answer. I went out to the range, got a bucket of balls, and started hitting. Mark Fry, the teacher, showed up and watched me hit three balls. He told me to move my hands forward at address and just hit it. Hallelujah, I hit three perfect shots in a row. As I looked up to have praise heaped on me by Mark, he was already ten yards away, walking toward the pro shop.

I yelled at him, “Hey, don’t you want to watch me? My half-hour isn’t up.”

“You’re cured,” he yelled back. “The other 29 minutes are B.S. anyway. Pay in the pro shop.”

Checking my score card.

I started playing for knee for fun, without a thought that it might be a metaphor for me. As I've written and reread these pages, it dawns on me that I've been playing for knee my entire life...for the approbation of my father and my boyhood buddies, for the approval of friends and family, for recognition by the golf pros and the golf public, and to satisfy my own self-image.

I draw a profound life-lesson from this: If you want to win approval in golf or life, you equally have to take the risk of losing and you have to be strong enough to suffer the consequences of defeat, especially the loss of self. Losses teach us more than wins, and the lessons are invaluable. I have learned that each setback is actually a test of strength and an obstacle to overcome.

For success, the game requires the same personal approach and traits that life does. Dedication and drive. Self-worth and self-confidence. Commitment to work and practice, never giving up, and becoming the best that you can be. Learning to manage yourself and your abilities and the course. Seeking and working constantly to improve. Observing the rules, written and unwritten, with integrity and honesty. Winning or losing with grace, dignity, sportsmanship and an eye to the future. Learning from your mistakes, and using the experience to your advantage.

In the final analysis, golf is only a game, even for the professionals who make their living playing it seriously. They learn to take the quirks of the game and the funny moments in stride. Again, life teaches the same lessons. Reality-based perspective and a sense of humor are vital.

Golf is a child's game made difficult by adults. In retrospect, I've loved it because it is a game for children, simple and fun and absorbing. I've always been captured by its magical quality. That's how I started. For me it has been made difficult by adults, and I am the adult who made it difficult for myself. I let it get the best of me.

When you expect too much, when your focus becomes too intense, the game loses the joy of innocence. Too much of a good thing is not a good thing. Life requires better balance than golf does; golf is simply a recreational part of life.

They say that everything is a trade-off with everything else. That certainly applies to golf. It temporarily defeated me and affected my life, but it has also given me much in the way of good friends, great fun, and a lot more. Through golf, I have traveled all over the country, been to the best places, and, most importantly, learned about myself and my place in the grand scheme of things. The game has given me an education in what to do...and what not to do. Golf indirectly put me in position to meet my wife, Bev. Through Beverly and golf, I was introduced to the Buffinis, Brian, Coach Judy, and the means to a better me and a better life. And it keeps getting better and better.

If it helps you find your smile, then golf and its humorous aspects are not so trivial. Because your smile is one of the most important elements of your life.

It has been demonstrated that the Great Scorer in the Pearly Gates Country Club has a sense of humor. Why else would He have someone say to me, "Better you should ask God why He gave you so many gifts" **on a golf course**. He must smile at the antics of golfers, wouldn't you think?

We're about at the end of the round. I'm approaching the time when I'll start to notice my skills eroding. I suppose I'll end up happy to shoot my age, and I'd like to get one or two more holes-in-one, God willing. And I have to stop automatically pressing...in golf matches and in every area of my life. I hope that as I get worse with age as a golfer, I get better as a person.

If you're ever in my area, let's play a round...for knee.

Acknowledgements

Brian Buffini

You threw me a lifeline and made me climb it. You pulled me up when I was down and tired. You saved my life. Thanks for being a true friend.

Mort Keilty

This book is yours as well as mine. Thank you for your advice and work on it. I hope you are as proud of it as I am. It's also great that two old guys have become friends in the process.

Coach Judy Hummerich

You guided me well and helped me see the way. Thank you for your caring direction and support.

Gary Buffini

You have been a quiet friend and a wonderful influence.

Mom and Dad

You both gave me life and shaped me. Dad, you are my model. Mom, you taught me to love. From you both I learned the value of family.

To order, copy this page and send it in.

To order additional copies of the book:

GOLF & me is available at special quantity discounts for bulk purchases for sales promotions, premiums or educational use. Special books or book excerpts also can be created to fit specific needs. For details, write: **Providence Systems, Inc.,**
6349 Palomar Oaks Court, Carlsbad, CA 92009

ISBN 0-9715638-2-9 **$22.50** U.S.

Payable in U.S. funds only. Postage & handling: U.S./Can. $5.00 for one book, $1.00 for each additional book. International: $8.00 for one book, $1.00 for each additional book. We accept Visa, MC, AMEX, Discover, checks ($15.00 fee for returned checks) and money orders. No cash/COD. Call 800-945-3485 or mail your orders to:
Providence Systems, Inc., 6349 Palomar Oaks Court, Carlsbad, CA 92009

Bill my credit card ______________________________exp. __________

Visa _______ MC ______ AMEX _____ Discover________

Signature ____

Bill to ______________________________ Book Total $_____

Address ____________________________

City ___________ST ____ZIP ________ Applicable sales tax $ ____

Phone No. __________________________ Postage & handling $ ____

Ship to: ____________________________

Address ____________________________ Total amount due $ ____

City ___________ST ____ZIP _______

Please allow 4-6 weeks for U.S. delivery. International orders allow 6-8 weeks.
This offer is subject to change without notice.